MEDICARE PART D
AND PRESCRIPTION DRUGS

HEALTH CARE ISSUES, COSTS, ACCESS

Additional books in this series can be found on Nova's website
under the Series tab.

Additional E-books in this series can be found on Nova's website
under the E-books tab.

HEALTH CARE ISSUES, COSTS, ACCESS

MEDICARE PART D AND PRESCRIPTION DRUGS

JOSHUA L. DAVIES
AND
BENJAMIN A. MASON
EDITORS

Nova Science Publishers, Inc.
New York

LIBRARY OF CONGRESS CATALOGING-IN-PUBLICATION DATA

Medicare Part D and prescription drugs / editors, Joshua L. Davies and
Benjamin A. Mason.
  p. ; cm.
Includes index.
ISBN 978-1-61122-899-1 (hardcover)
1. Pharmaceutical services insurance--United States. 2. Medicare. I.
Davies, Joshua L. II. Mason, Benjamin A.
[DNLM: 1. Medicare Part D. 2. Prescription Drugs. WT 31]
HG9391.5.U6M43 2011
368.4'26--dc22
                           2010047025

Published by Nova Science Publishers, Inc. ✛ *New York*

CONTENTS

PREFACE

The Medicare Prescription Drug, Improvement, and Modernization Act of 2003 established an outpatient voluntary prescription drug benefit under a new Medicare Part D. Drug coverage is provided through private prescription drug plans (PDPs), which offer only prescription drug coverage, or through Medicare Advantage (MA) prescription drug plans. This new book examines Medicare Part D and prescription drug issues; the effects of using generic drugs on Medicare's prescription drug spending; and Medicare Part D and its impact in the nursing home sector.

Chapter 1- The Medicare Prescription Drug, Improvement, and Modernization Act of 2003 (MMA, P.L. 108-173) established an outpatient voluntary prescription drug benefit under a new Medicare Part D, effective January 1, 2006. Drug coverage is provided through private prescription drug plans (PDPs), which offer only prescription drug coverage, or through Medicare Advantage (MA) prescription drug plans (MA-PDs), which offer prescription drug coverage that is integrated with the health care coverage they provide to Medicare beneficiaries under Part C. These private plans bear some of the financial risk for drug costs; however, federal subsidies covering the bulk of the risk are provided to encourage participation.

Chapter 2- In 2006, Medicare began offering outpatient prescription drug benefits to senior citizens and people with disabilities in a program called Part D. Unlike other Medicare benefits covered under the traditional fee-for-service program—in which providers are paid an administratively determined price for each covered service (or bundle of services) they provide—prices in Part D are not set by the government. Instead, private plans deliver the drug benefit

and negotiate their own drug prices while competing with each other for
enrollees.

Chapter 3- In 2006, the Medicare Payment Advisory Commission
(MedPAC) contracted with Harvard Medical School to explore how Medicare
Part D's introduction changed the operations of long-term care pharmacies
(LTCPs) and nursing homes, as well as implications of those changes for
nursing home residents. Based on interviews conducted across a broad range
of stakeholders (nursing homes, LTCPs, Part D plans, financial analysts
covering the LTCP sector, consultant pharmacists, physicians working in
nursing homes, and advocates for nursing home residents), the June 2007
report offered a snapshot of this sector's transition to Part D. In 2009,
MedPAC contracted with Harvard Medical School to update this work by
conducting a second round of stakeholder interviews, the findings of which are
detailed in this report. The report briefly updates changes in the LTCP industry
since early 2007 and describes the recent impact of Part D focusing on: Part D
plan assignment and selection; PDP formularies and drug coverage; mechanics
of dispensing medications to nursing home residents under Part D; and the
impact of Part D on drug utilization and health outcomes for nursing home
residents.

Chapter 4- Medicare Part D requires plans to establish a formulary that
lists the drugs that the plan agrees to cover and at what level of cost sharing.
Although the original standard" benefit package with 25 percent cost to offer a
benefit with tiered cost sharing. Plans typically use this flexibility to offer
different levels of cost sharing for generic, preferred, and non-preferred drugs.
A growing number of plans include an additional "specialty" Most plans use
flat copayments for most oftier for very high their tiers (*e.g.,* $5 for generics,
$30 for preferred brands), but variable coinsurance for specialty tiers (*e.g.,* 25
percent of the drug's cost).

In: Medicare Part D and Prescription Drugs   ISBN: 978-1-61122-899-1
Editors: J. L. Davies and B. A. Mason   ©2011 Nova Science Publishers, Inc.

Chapter 1

MEDICARE PART D PRESCRIPTION DRUG BENEFIT

Patricia A. Davis

SUMMARY

The Medicare Prescription Drug, Improvement, and Modernization Act of 2003 (MMA, P.L. 108-173) established an outpatient voluntary prescription drug benefit under a new Medicare Part D, effective January 1, 2006. Drug coverage is provided through private prescription drug plans (PDPs), which offer only prescription drug coverage, or through Medicare Advantage (MA) prescription drug plans (MA-PDs), which offer prescription drug coverage that is integrated with the health care coverage they provide to Medicare beneficiaries under Part C. These private plans bear some of the financial risk for drug costs; however, federal subsidies covering the bulk of the risk are provided to encourage participation.

At a minimum, plans offer "standard coverage" or alternative coverage with actuarially equivalent benefits. They may also offer enhanced benefits. All plans are required to meet certain minimum requirements, including those related to beneficiary protections. However, there are significant differences among plans in terms of benefit design, drugs included on plan formularies (i.e., list of covered drugs), cost-sharing applicable for particular drugs, and monthly premiums. In general, beneficiaries can enroll in a plan, or change plan enrollment, when they first become eligible for Medicare or during the annual open enrollment period. In 2009, beneficiaries could choose from among close to 50 PDP options in each of the 34 PDP regions. As plan sponsors may change their plan offerings from year to year, beneficiaries need to carefully review their plan choices annually to make sure that the plans they select continue to meet their needs.

A major focus of the drug benefit is the enhanced coverage provided to low-income individuals who enroll in Part D. Persons with incomes below 150% of poverty and assets below certain limits may receive assistance with some portion of their premiums and cost-sharing charges. Individuals enrolled in both Medicare and Medicaid (dual-eligibles), as well as certain other low-income enrollees, are enrolled in plans with premiums at or below the low-income subsidy level for the region. In recent years, the number of plans available to low-income subsidy recipients for no monthly premium has been declining.

In 2009, approximately 27 million beneficiaries are enrolled in either a PDP or a MA-PD, and over a third of them are receiving the low-income subsidy. In total, about 90% of Medicare beneficiaries have some form of drug coverage either through Medicare or other type of insurance. Total expenditures for Part D are projected to exceed $60 billion in 2009.

While early start-up issues with the Part D program have generally been resolved, some issues remain and others are emerging. Discussions regarding the overall structure of program benefits, costs to Medicare and beneficiaries, the availability of plans for low-income enrollees, and oversight of the program are likely to continue. This report will be updated as events warrant.

OVERVIEW

In January 2009, the Medicare prescription drug program began its fourth year of operation. The Medicare Prescription Drug, Improvement, and Modernization Act of 2003 (MMA, P.L. 108-173) created this voluntary outpatient prescription drug benefit under a new Medicare Part D, effective January 1, 2006. At that time, Medicare replaced Medicaid as the primary source of drug coverage for beneficiaries covered under both programs (called *dual eligibles*). Since the MMA's enactment, several statutes have modified or amended the Part D program. These statutes include the QI, TMA, and Abstinence Programs Extension and Hurricane Katrina Unemployment Relief Act of 2005 (P.L. 109-91); the Tax Relief and Health Care Act of 2006

(TRHCA, P.L. 109-432); and the Medicare Improvements for Patients and Providers Act of 2008 (MIPPA, P.L. 110-275).[1]

Prescription drug coverage is provided through private prescription drug plans (PDPs), which offer only prescription drug coverage, or through Medicare Advantage (MA) prescription drug plans (MA-PDs), which offer prescription drug coverage that is integrated with the health care coverage they provide to Medicare beneficiaries under Part C. The MMA also provides for subsidy payments to sponsors of qualified retiree prescription drug plans (the retiree drug subsidy) to encourage retention of non-Part D employer-sponsored benefits. In 2009, approximately 27 million beneficiaries are enrolled in either a PDP or a MA-PD and another 6 million are enrolled in a subsidized retiree prescription drug plan. In total, about 90% of Medicare beneficiaries have some form of drug coverage.

A major focus of the drug benefit is the enhanced coverage provided to low-income individuals who enroll in Part D. Individuals with incomes below 150% of the federal poverty limit and limited assets are eligible for the low-income subsidy (LIS). The LIS reduces beneficiaries' out-of-pocket spending by paying for all or some of the Part D monthly premium and annual deductible, and limits drug copayments to a nominal price. Persons with the lowest incomes receive the highest level of benefits. In 2009, approximately 9.6 million beneficiaries (about one-third of Part D enrollees) are receiving the low-income subsidy.

The Part D program relies on private plans to provide coverage and to bear some of the financial risk for drug costs; federal subsidies covering the bulk of the risk are provided to encourage participation. While all plans must meet certain minimum requirements, there are significant variations among them in benefit design, including differences in premiums, drugs included on plan formularies (i.e., list of covered drugs), and cost-sharing applicable for particular drugs. In 2009, there are a total of 1,689 PDPs and 2,039 MA-PDs nationwide.

PROGRAM FINANCING

The MMA established within the Supplementary Medical Insurance (SMI) trust fund the Medicare Prescription Drug Account to be used in conjunction with the Part D prescription drug program (see **Table 1**). The Part D program is primarily funded through general revenues. The appropriation language adopted for the Part D account allows substantial flexibility in the amount of general revenues available to the account. This flexibility eliminates the need for a contingency reserve; as a result, assets in the Part D account are generally low.

Expenditures

According to the 2009 Annual Trustees Report, during calendar year (CY) 2008, total Part D expenditures were approximately $49.3 billion.[2] This amount included the combined costs of prescription drugs provided by Part D plans to enrollees and Medicare payments to employer-sponsored retiree health plans ($49.0 billion). The remaining $0.3 billion in expenditures covered federal administrative expenses, including expenses incurred by the Department of Health and Human Services (HHS), the Social Security Administration (SSA), and the Department of the Treasury in administering Part D. Such duties include making payments to Part D plans and implementing fraud and abuse control activities.

Revenues

The major sources of revenue for the Part D account include general revenues, beneficiary premiums, and state contributions. Total Part D revenues in CY2008 were $49.4 billion.

General Revenues and Beneficiary Premiums

General revenues are transferred from the Treasury to the Part D Account on an as-needed basis to cover the portion of program expenditures funded by federal subsidies. In CY2008, contributions received from the general fund of the Treasury amounted to $37.3 billion, which accounted for about 76% of total Part D revenue.

Beneficiaries may have their premiums deducted from their Social Security or other federal benefit payments; these are then forwarded to Part D plans on their behalf. Alternatively, they can pay their premiums directly to the Part D plans. In 2008, $1.9 billion in premium amounts were withheld from Social Security benefit checks or other federal benefit payments. Another $3.1 billion in premiums were paid directly to the plans by beneficiaries.

Beneficiary premiums accounted for approximately 10% of revenues (see "Premiums" and "Part D Plans: Payment and Participation").

State Contributions

After Part D drug coverage and low-income subsidies became available in 2006, Medicaid is no longer the primary payer of drug costs for full-benefit dual-eligible beneficiaries. However, MMA contained a provision (labeled by some as the "clawback provision") that requires states to pay the Part D account in the SMI trust fund a portion of the costs that they would have incurred for this population if they were still the primary payer. Starting in 2006, states paid 90% of these estimated costs. This percentage phases down over a 10-year period to 75% in 2015. In 2008, these state payments amounted to $7.1 billion, or about 14% of revenues.

Table 1. Statement of Operations of Part D Account, CY2008 (in millions)

Total Assets at Beginning of Year	$801.0
Revenues	**$49,371.5**
Premiums from Enrollees	4,998.6
Premiums deducted from Social Security checks	1,873.3
Premiums paid directly to plans	3,125.3
Government Contributions	37,255.4
Prescription drug benefits	36,979.3
Administrative expenses	276.1
Payments from States	7,104.8
Interest on Investments	12.7
Expenditures	**$49,261.2**
Benefit Payments	48,982.1
Federal Administrative Expenses	**279.1**

Source: Table III.C17, 2009 Annual Report of the Boards of Trustees of the Federal Hospital Insurance and Federal Supplementary Insurance Trust Funds.

Note: Totals may not add due to rounding.

Estimated Program Expenditures

The growth in prescription drug spending under Part D has been lower than projected at the beginning of the program. Actual prescription drug costs for 2006 and 2007 were significantly lower than the costs estimated in the bids submitted by plans for the 2006 plan year, and somewhat lower than the trustees' estimates in their 2007 report. This may have occurred, in part, because the actual rebates that drug plans received from manufacturers and the use of generic drugs were higher than expected.

Medicare expenditures for the Part D drug benefit were approximately $47 billion in CY2006 and are expected to exceed $60 billion in 2009. The 2009 Medicare Trustees Report projects that total Part D expenditures, based on intermediate estimates, will reach $140.8 billion in 2018. The per capita benefits are projected to increase from $1,517 in 2008 to $3,177 in 2018. These cost estimates have been adjusted downward from the 2008 report, primarily due to an expected decline in the number of new drug products expected to reach the market. Additionally, the trustees are projecting higher income from premiums due to an expected change in methodology used to calculate risk scores.[3] Part D expenditures are still, however, projected to increase rapidly over the next ten years due to further expected increases in Part D enrollment and cost growth rates that are expected to exceed those for other categories of medical spending. The Trustees Report cautions that there is a high level of uncertainty surrounding these cost projections, as there is still little experience with this new benefit upon which to base conclusions.

ELIGIBILITY

General Medicare Population

In general, anyone entitled to Medicare Part A and/or enrolled in Part B is eligible to enroll in a Medicare prescription drug plan. The individual must also permanently reside in the service area of a PDP. Anyone living abroad or who is incarcerated is not eligible, as he or she cannot meet this requirement. For most people, joining Part D is voluntary. (Dual-eligible beneficiaries are automatically signed up for Part D, as described in "LIS Enrollment.") Beneficiaries cannot be denied coverage for health reasons or for high utilization of prescription drugs.

As of February 2009, of the 45.2 Medicare beneficiaries eligible for Part D, approximately 26.7 million are enrolled in either a stand-alone prescription drug plan (17.5 million) or in a Medicare Advantage or other Medicare health plan with drug coverage (9.2 million). An additional 6.0 million have prescription drug coverage through a former employer that is receiving a federal subsidy for a portion of the coverage. About 8.2 million have drug coverage through another source, such as the Federal Employees Health Benefits program or TRICARE. Approximately 4.5 million beneficiaries (about 10%) have no drug coverage (see Table 2).

Table 2. Total Medicare Beneficiaries with Prescription Drug Coverage, 2009 (in millions)

Description	2009	Percent of Eligible
Medicare Beneficiaries Eligible for Part D	**45.2**	**100.0%**
Medicare Part D	**26.7**	**58.9**
Stand-Alone PDP	17.5	38.6
MA with Drug Coverage	9.0	19.8
Other Plan Types	0.2	0.4
Medicare Retiree Drug Subsidy (RDS)	**6.0**	**13.2**
Other Drug Coverage	**8.2**	**18.0**
TRICARE	1.0	2.1
FEHB Retiree Coverage	1.0	2.2
Veterans Affairs Coverage	1.6	3.5
Active Workers with Medicare Secondary Payer	1.8	4.0
Multiple Sources of Creditable Coverage	0.8	1.7
Retiree Coverage (Not RDS)	1.5	3.3
Medigap and Other Individual Insurance	0.2	0.4
State Pharmaceutical Assistance Programs	<0,1	<0.1
Indian Health Service Coverage	<0.1	<0.1
Other Sources	0.3	0.7
Total Beneficiaries with Drug Coverage	**40.8**	**90.1**

Source: CMS, February 2009, http://www.cms.hhs.gov/ PrescriptionDrug CovGen In/01_Overview.asp. Note: Totals may not add due to rounding.

**Table 3. LIS-Eligible Medicare Beneficiaries with Drug Coverage,
2009 (in millions)**

Description	Total LIS-Eligible Beneficiaries
Total Beneficiaries Eligible for Low-Income Subsidy	**12.5**
Less: Drug Coverage from Medicare	**9.6**
CMS-Deemed Full Dual Eligibles	6.3
CMS-Deemed MSP and SSI Recipients	1.8
LIS Approved and Not Deemed	1.5
Less: Drug Coverage from Former Employer	**<0.1**
Less: Additional Sources of Creditable Drug Coverage	**0.4**
Veterans Affairs (VA) Coverage	0.4
Indian Health Service Coverage	<0.1
Less: Anticipated Facilitated Enrollments	**<0.1**
Total Remaining LIS-Eligible Beneficiaries	**2.3**

Source: CMS, February 2009, http://www.cms.hhs.gov/ PrescriptionDrugCov GenIn/
01_Overview.asp.

Eligibility for Low-Income Assistance

Some beneficiaries with limited income and resources may qualify for
assistance with a portion of their Part D premiums, cost-sharing, and other out-
of-pocket expenses. As of February 2009, an estimated 12.5 million Medicare
beneficiaries are eligible for low-income subsidies (LIS). Of these, nearly 9.6
million are receiving subsidies because they automatically qualify as full dual
eligibles, Medicare Savings Program (MSP) recipients,[4] or Supplemental
Security Income (SSI) recipients.[5] Another 1.5 million beneficiaries receive
low-income subsidies because they applied and were determined eligible.
Finally, 2.3 million low-income Medicare beneficiaries are thought to be
eligible for low-income subsidies but are not receiving them (see Table 3).

Full-Subsidy Eligible Individuals

Certain groups of Medicare beneficiaries automatically qualify (and are
deemed eligible) for the full low-income subsidy. Dual eligibles who qualify
for Medicaid based on their income and assets are automatically deemed
eligible for Medicare prescription drug low-income subsidies. Additionally,

those who receive premium and/or cost-sharing assistance from Medicaid through the Medicare savings programs, plus those eligible for SSI cash assistance, are automatically deemed eligible for low-income subsidies and need not apply for them. This group includes all eligible persons who (1) have incomes below 135% of the federal poverty level ($14,621 for an individual and $19,670 for a couple in 2009)[6] and (2) have resources in 2009 below $8,100 for an individual and $12,910 for a couple (increased each year by the percentage increase in the consumer price index, or CPI).[7] (See **Table 4**.)

CMS deems individuals automatically eligible for LIS effective as of the first day of the month that the individual attains the qualifying status (e.g., becomes eligible for Medicaid, MSP, or SSI). The end date is, at a minimum, through the end of the calendar year within which the individual becomes eligible. Beneficiaries who are deemed LIS-eligible for any month during the period of July through December of one year are deemed eligible through the end of the following calendar year. CMS changes an individual's deemed status mid-year only when such a change qualifies the beneficiary for a reduced co-payment obligation.

Eligibility for the LIS is not always continuous from year to year. For example, LIS beneficiaries who lose eligibility for Medicaid, MSP, or SSI during the year are not automatically qualified to receive the LIS the next year. CMS notifies these individuals in September of each year that their LIS-deemed status will end on December 31 of that year. Such individuals may reapply for the LIS, as they may qualify for the LIS through the application process (see "LIS Enrollment"). According to CMS, 447,000 beneficiaries lost their deemed status between 2008 and 2009.

Other Subsidy-Eligible Individuals

Other individuals with limited income and resources who do not automatically qualify may apply for the low-income subsidy and have their eligibility determined by either the Social Security Administration or their state Medicaid agency. This group includes all other persons who (1) are enrolled in a PDP plan or MA-PD plan, (2) have incomes below 150% of poverty ($16,245 for an individual and $21,855 for a couple in 2009), and (3) have assets in 2009 below $12,510 for an individual and $25,010 for a couple (increased in future years by the percentage increase in the CPI). According to SSA,[8] in 2008, approximately 17% of low-income subsidy applicants who were determined ineligible would have qualified based on income alone, but had excess assets.

Table 4. Overview of How Medicare Beneficiaries Qualify for LIS

Eligibility	People with Medicare and Medicaid benefits	Basis	Data Source	Changes During the Year
Full Subsidy Eligible	• Full Medicaid benefits • Partial Dual (QMB-only, SLMB-only, QI) SSI benefits	Automatically qualify	State Files SSA	Qualify for a full calendar year • Generally only favorable changes will occur
Other Subsidy Eligible	Limited Income and Resources	Must apply	SSA (almost all) or states	• Some events can impact status throughout the year • Extra help can increase, decrease or terminate

Source: CMS, August 7, 2008, memo from Anthony Culotta to Part D Plan Sponsors, on Re-Determination of Low-Income Subsidy Eligibility for 2009.

An individual who applies and is determined eligible for the LIS is eligible effective the first day of the month in which the individual submitted an application. In most cases, this means that LIS status is applied retroactively. For example, if a beneficiary is already enrolled in a Part D plan, the Part D sponsor must take steps to ensure that the beneficiary has been reimbursed for any premiums or cost-sharing the member had paid that should have been covered by the subsidy.

Individual LIS determinations are made for a period not to exceed 12 months. After that time, if the individual is found ineligible, the subsequent end date would be established by the agency that made the decision (either the state or SSA). The end date is always the last day of a calendar month but may occur in any month of the year.

PART D BENEFIT STRUCTURE

Medicare law sets out a standard prescription drug benefit structure. Plan sponsors may, however, offer different benefit designs and cost-sharing requirements, as long as they meet certain specifications. Under the standard benefit structure, with some exceptions, over the course of the year a beneficiary is responsible for paying (1) a monthly premium, (2) an annual deductible, and (3) co-payments or co-insurance for drug purchases. Additionally, for a certain period called the "coverage gap," beneficiaries may be responsible for the full cost of their drugs. The actual costs to beneficiaries under Part D will vary and depend upon the benefit structure and coverage offered by a particular plan, the costs and amount of drugs needed, and whether the beneficiary receives some form of assistance.

Premiums

The majority of beneficiaries enrolled in Part D pay monthly premiums for Part D coverage. On average, beneficiary premiums represent roughly 25.5% of the cost of basic coverage. However, the amount of the premiums can vary by the plan selected.

Beneficiary premiums are based on the average bid submitted by drug plans for basic benefits (the base beneficiary premium) for each year and are adjusted to reflect the difference between the plan's standardized bid amount and the nationwide average bid. (In 2009, the base beneficiary monthly premium is $30.36. See **Table 5.**) Thus, beneficiaries in plans with higher costs for standard coverage face higher than average premiums for such coverage, while enrollees in lower cost plans pay lower than average premiums for such coverage. Additionally, enrollees in MA-PD plans may see lower premiums if their plans buy down the Part D premium.[9] The monthly premium is the same for all persons enrolled in the plan (except for those receiving low-income subsidies or those subject to a late enrollment penalty).

Table 5. Premium Trends, 2006-2009

Premium	2006	2007	2008	2009
Base Premium[a]	$32.20	$27.35	$27.93	$30.36
Average PDP Premium[b]	26.03	27.39	29.86	37.27
Average MA-PDP Premium[b]	12.08	10.35	11.97	15.15

Source: CMS, "Release of the Part D National Average Monthly Bid Amount, the Medicare Part D Base Beneficiary Premium, the Part D Regional Low-Income Premium Subsidy Amounts, and the Medicare Advantage Regional Benchmarks," August 15, 2006, August 13, 2007, and August 14, 2008; Medicare Payment Advisory Commission, "Report to Congress, Medicare Payment Policy", March 2009, March 2008, March 2007.
a. The base premium represents 25.5% of the national average monthly bid amount for basic coverage.
b. Average PDP and MA-PD premiums for 2006 and 2007 were weighted by actual enrollment in each plan. The average premiums for 2008 and 2009 were weighted by estimated enrollments.

Qualified Drug Coverage

Under Medicare Part D, PDPs and MA-PDs are required to offer a minimum set of benefits. This minimum set, referred to as "qualified coverage," may include either the standard prescription drug coverage established by Medicare or alternative prescription drug coverage with benefits that are at least of equivalent dollar value (actuarially equivalent). Plans also have the option of offering "enhanced coverage," which exceeds the value of the defined standard coverage.

Standard Prescription Drug Coverage

The Part D standard benefit includes a *deductible* paid by the beneficiary ($295 in 2009); 75% of costs paid by the program and 25% of costs paid by the beneficiary up to the *initial coverage limit* ($2,700 in 2009); 100% of costs paid by the beneficiary for drug spending falling in the *coverage gap* (between $2,700 and $6,153.75 in 2009);[10] and all costs paid by program over the *catastrophic threshold* ($6,153.75 in 2009) except for nominal beneficiary cost-sharing.[11] (See **Figure 1** and **Table 7**.)

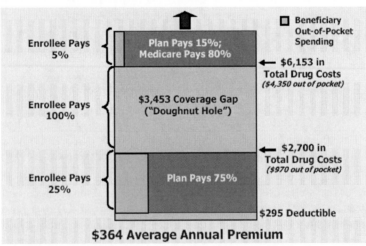

Source: Kaiser Family Foundation, The Medicare Prescription Drug Benefit Fact Sheet, March 2009,

Notes: Annual premium amount based on $30.36 national average monthly beneficiary premium. Amounts are rounded to nearest dollar.

Figure 1. Standard Medicare Prescription Drug Benefit, 2009

Each year, the deductible, co-payments, and coverage thresholds are increased by the annual percentage increase in average per-capita aggregate expenditures for covered outpatient drugs for Medicare beneficiaries for the 12-month period ending in July of the previous year.

Alternative Prescription Drug Coverage

Plans may offer different benefit structures, providing they have the same actuarial value as the standard benefit. For example, plans may eliminate the deductible but have cost-sharing requirements higher than the 25% amount under basic standard coverage. They may also use tiered cost-sharing—for example, design a benefit structure under which generics have lower cost-sharing than higher-cost brand-name drugs.

In 2009, only 10% of PDPs and 5% of MA-PDs nationwide offered the standard drug benefit,[12] while 37% of PDPs and 8% of MA-PDs offered plans that were actuarially equivalent. In 2008, 17% of PDP enrollees and 1% of MA-PD enrollees were in defined standard benefit plans. In the same year, 61% of PDP enrollees and 6% of MA-PD enrollees were enrolled in actuarially equivalent plans.

In 2009, 55% of PDPs and 88% of MA-PDs offered plans with a zero deductible.[13] The percentage of beneficiaries enrolled in a PDP with no deductible grew from 72% in 2006 to 75% in 2008, and for MA-PDs from 89% to 92%.

Enhanced Coverage

Plans may also offer enhanced coverage that exceeds the value of defined standard coverage. This coverage includes both basic coverage as well as some supplemental benefits that increase the actuarial value of the package. For example, these supplemental benefits may include reductions in cost sharing and/or some coverage in the coverage gap.

A PDP-sponsor cannot offer an enhanced plan unless it also offers a basic plan in the service area. MA organizations offering MA coordinated care plans are required to offer at least one plan in the service area with drug coverage. The drug coverage can be either basic coverage or enhanced coverage with no premium for the supplemental benefits.

In 2009, 53% of PDPs offered enhanced coverage, while 88% of MA-PDs offered these types of plans.[14] As of October 2008, 23% of PDP enrollees were in enhanced plans, while 93% of MA-PD enrollees were in such plans.

The Coverage Gap

A unique feature of the Medicare Part D drug benefit is the coverage gap—a period in coverage in which Part D enrollees are required to pay 100% of total drug costs until they reach the catastrophic coverage level. The coverage gap was included in the benefit structure because the cost of providing continuous coverage would have exceeded the budgetary limit when the program was established.

CMS estimates that 31.7% (8.3 million) of Part D enrollees reached the initial coverage limit of their drug plans in 2007.[15] About 23.9% of non-LIS enrollees reached the initial coverage limit, compared with 43.7% of LIS enrollees. Approximately 36.3% of enrollees in PDPs (which include a large proportion of LIS enrollees) reached the coverage gap, compared with 21.3% of those in MA-PDs.

In 2009, nearly all Part D plans include a gap in coverage. The availability and generosity of gap coverage varies widely across Part D plans. About 25% of PDPs (416 plans) offer some type of gap coverage (down from 29% in 2008).[16] Approximately 51% of MA-PD plans offer some gap coverage (1,076 plans), the same share as in 2008 and twice the share of PDPs with gap coverage. Monthly premiums for PDPs that provide gap coverage are about double those of PDPs with no gap coverage in 2009. About 10.9% (2.9 million) of enrollees who reached the coverage gap were responsible for the full cost of their drugs, either because they were not LIS-eligible or they were not enrolled in plans with gap coverage.

In 2009, as in previous years, the majority of plans offering gap coverage cover only generic drugs during the gap, and most cover only a subset of the generics listed in their formularies. Full gap coverage for brand-name and generic drugs does not currently exist in the PDP market.[17]

In addition to determining whether one is eligible to receive the low-income subsidy, CMS offers enrollees a number of other suggestions for avoiding or delaying the gap and for saving money while in the gap. These suggestions include switching to generic,[18] over-the-counter, mail order, or other lower cost drugs when possible; looking at State Pharmaceutical Assistance Programs for which one may qualify;[19] exploring national and community-based charitable programs that may offer assistance; and looking into Pharmaceutical Assistance Programs (also sometimes called Patient Assistance Programs) that may be offered by the manufacturers of the drugs taken.[20] Additionally, CMS suggests that beneficiaries continue using their Medicare drug plan cards even when in the coverage gap. This helps to ensure that beneficiaries pay the drug plan's discounted *negotiated prices* and that *out-of-pocket expenses* count toward catastrophic coverage.

Access to Negotiated Prices

Part D plan sponsors (or the pharmaceutical benefit managers [PBMs] they have contracted with) negotiate prices with drug manufacturers, wholesalers, and pharmacies.[21] All plans are required to provide beneficiaries with access to these negotiated prices for covered Part D drugs. This access must be provided even when no Part D benefits are payable because the beneficiary has not met the deductible or the beneficiary is in the coverage gap. Negotiated prices are to take into account negotiated price concessions for covered drugs.[22] Such price concessions include discounts, direct or indirect subsidies, rebates, and other direct or indirect remunerations. The plan's negotiated price may reflect the same prices that a health plan or PBM would get for its commercially insured members, or it may be different.

The prices for drugs on a plan's formulary may be found on the www.medicare.gov website. Beneficiaries can also compare prices for different plans in their area. The net prices, including price concessions, charged to Part D plans by drug manufactures are reported to CMS; however, they are not made public.

True Out-Of-Pocket (TrOOP) Expenses

Under a standard plan design, beneficiaries must incur a certain level of out-of-pocket costs ($4,350 in 2009) before catastrophic protection begins. These include costs that are incurred for the deductible, cost-sharing, or benefits not paid because they fall in the coverage gap. Costs are counted as incurred, and thus treated as true out-of-pocket (TrOOP) costs only if they are paid by the individual (or by another family member on behalf of the individual), paid on behalf of a low-income individual under the subsidy provisions, or paid under a State Pharmaceutical Assistance Program. Incurred costs do not include amounts for which no benefits are provided—for example, because a drug is excluded under a particular plan's formulary. Additional payments that do not count toward TrOOP include Part D premiums and coverage by other insurance, including group health plans, workers' compensation, Part D plans' supplemental or enhanced benefits, or other third parties.

Premium Subsidies for Low-Income Populations

Premium subsidies are available for both full-subsidy-eligible and other subsidy-eligible persons. The premium subsidy will vary based on the subsidy level for which the beneficiary qualifies.

Full-Subsidy-Eligible Individuals

Low-income beneficiaries who are eligible for the full premium subsidy may enroll in a benchmark plan without paying any premium. A Part D PDP qualifies as a "benchmark plan" if it offers basic Part D coverage with premiums equal to or lower than the regional low-income premium subsidy amount. (See "Availability of Low-Income Plans.") However, if a beneficiary selects a plan with a premium higher than the benchmark, the beneficiary is liable for the additional costs.

Other Subsidy-Eligible Individuals

Partial-subsidy-eligible individuals receive a sliding scale premium subsidy ranging from 100% to 25% of the premium subsidy amount, as specified in **Table 6**.

Table 6. Sliding Scale Premium for Partial-Subsidy-Eligible Individuals

FPL and Assets	Percentage of Premium Subsidy Amount
Income up to 135% FPL, and with assets that do not exceed the calendar year resource limits for individuals or couples.	100%
Income above 135% FPL but at or below 140% FPL, and with assets that do not exceed the calendar year resource limits for individuals or couples.	75%
Income above 140% FPL but at or below 145% FPL, and with assets that do not exceed the calendar year resource limits for individuals or couples.	50%
Income above 145% FPL but below 150% FPL, and with assets that do not exceed the calendar year resource limits for individuals or couples.	25%

Source: Prescription Drug Benefit Manual, Chapter 13—Premium and Cost-Sharing Subsidies for Low-Income Individuals, Rev. 7, 11-21-08.

Table 7. Part D Standard Benefits, 2009 (by per capita drug spending category)

Total drug spending (dollar ranges)	All Beneficiaries		Subsidy-Eligible Individuals			
			Full-Subsidy Eligible		Other Subsidy Eligible	
	Paid by Part D	Paid by Enrollee	Paid by Part D	Paid by Enrollee	Paid by Part D	Paid by Enrollee
$0 up to $295 Deductible	0%	$295	$295	0	$235	$60
Between Deductible and Initial Coverage Limit ($295.01-$2,700)	75%	25%	100% less enrollee cost-sharing	Institutionalized duals: $0 Duals under 100% of poverty: $1.10/$3.20[a] Others: $2.40/$6.00[b]	85%	15%
Coverage Gap Between Initial Coverage Limit ($2,700.01) and Catastrophic Trigger ($6,153.75)	0%	100%	100% less enrollee cost-sharing	Institutionalized duals: $0 Duals under 100% of poverty: $1.10/$3.20[a] Others: $2.40/$6.00[b]	85%	15%
Over Catastrophic Trigger ($6,153.76 and over)	95%	5%	100%	$0	100% less enrollee cost sharing	$2.40/$6.00[b]

Source: CMS, Announcement of CY2009 Medicare Advantage Capitation Rates and Medicare Advantage and Part D Payment Policies, http://www.cms.hhs. gov/ Medicare AdvtgSpecRate Stats/ Downloads/ Announcement2009.pdf.

a. $1.10 per prescription for generic or preferred drugs that are multiple source drugs; $3.20 per prescription for other drugs.

b. $2.40 per prescription for generic or preferred drugs that are multiple source drugs; $6.00 per prescription for other drugs.

Cost-Sharing Subsidies for Low-Income Population

Cost-sharing subsides for LIS enrollees are linked to the standard prescription drug coverage. Full-subsidy eligibles have no deductible, minimal cost sharing during the initial coverage period and coverage gap, and no cost-sharing over the catastrophic threshold. Additionally, full-benefit dual eligibles who are residents of medical institutions or nursing facilities have no cost-sharing. Other full-benefit dual-eligible individuals with incomes up to 100% of poverty have cost-sharing, for all costs up to the out-of-pocket threshold, of

$1.10 in 2009 for a generic drug prescription or preferred multiple source drug prescription and $3.20 in 2009 for any other drug prescription. All other full-subsidy-eligible individuals have cost-sharing for all costs up to the out-of-pocket threshold, of $2.40 in 2009 for a generic drug or preferred multiple source drug and $6.00 in 2009 for any other drug (see **Table 7**).

Partial-subsidy-eligible individuals have a $60 deductible in 2009, 15% coinsurance for all costs up to the catastrophic trigger level, and cost-sharing for costs above this level of $2.40 in 2009 for a generic drug prescription or preferred multiple source drug prescription and $6.00 in 2009 for any other drug prescription. Each year, the cost-sharing amounts for full-benefit dual eligibles below 100% of poverty are increased by the increase in the Consumer Price Index. The cost-sharing amounts for all other beneficiaries, and the deductible amount for other subsidy eligible individuals, are increased by the annual percentage increase in per-capita beneficiary expenditures for Part D-covered drugs.

DRUG COVERAGE

In order for a drug to be paid under Medicare's prescription drug benefit, it must be a drug that is covered under Part D and included in the formulary of an individual's Part D plan. The law defines covered Part D drugs as (1) outpatient prescription drugs approved by the Food and Drug Administration (FDA), and used for a medically accepted indication; (2) biological products that may be dispensed only upon a prescription and that are licensed under the Public Health Service (PHS) Act and produced at a licensed establishment; (3) insulin (including medical supplies associated with the injection of insulin); and (4) vaccines licensed under the PHS Act. Also included are drugs treated as being included in a plan's formulary as a result of a coverage determination or appeal.

A few drugs are excluded from Medicare coverage by law, including drugs specifically excluded from coverage under Medicaid. This exclusion applies to (1) benzodiazepines; (2) barbiturates; (3) drugs used for anorexia, weight loss, or weight gain; (4) fertility drugs; (5) drugs used for cosmetic purposes or hair growth; (6) drugs for symptomatic relief for coughs and colds; (7) prescription vitamins and minerals; and (8) covered drugs when the manufacturer requires, as a condition of sale, that associated tests be purchased exclusively from the manufacturer. In addition, drugs used for the treatment of sexual or erectile dysfunction are excluded, unless they are used to treat another condition for which the drug has been approved by the FDA (off-label uses for these drugs are not covered). However, for prescriptions dispensed on or after January 1, 2013, plans will be required to include benzodiazepines in their formularies. Barbiturates will also be required to be included in the formularies for the indication of epilepsy, cancer, or chronic mental health disorder.

If a state covers these excludable drugs for Medicaid beneficiaries, then it also must cover them for dual eligibles when they are medically necessary. Dual eligibles may therefore receive coverage from Medicaid for some drugs excluded from Medicare. Additionally, a Part D sponsor may elect to include one or more of these drugs in an enhanced Part D plan; however, no federal subsidy is available for the associated costs.

Drugs Covered by other Parts of Medicare

Part D drug plans are prohibited from covering drugs covered by other parts of Medicare. This includes prescription medications provided during a stay in a hospital or skilled nursing facility that are paid for by the Part A program, and in the limited circumstances when Part B covers prescription drugs. Part B-covered drugs include drugs that are not usually self-administered and are provided incident to a physician's professional services. These include such things as immunosuppressive drugs for persons who have had a Medicare-covered transplant; erythropoietin (anti-anemia drug) for persons with end-stage renal disease; oral anti-cancer drugs; drugs requiring administration via a nebulizer or infusion pump in the home; and certain vaccines (influenza, pneumococcal, and hepatitis B for intermediate- or high-risk persons).

Formularies

Prescription drug plans are permitted to operate formularies—lists of drugs that a plan chooses to cover and the terms under which they are covered. This means that plans can choose to cover some, but not all, FDA-approved prescription drugs.

A Part D sponsor's formulary must be developed and reviewed by a Pharmacy and Therapeutics Committee. The majority of the committee members are required to be practicing physicians or practicing pharmacists and must include clinical specialties that adequately represent the needs of beneficiaries. When developing and reviewing the formulary, the committee is to base clinical decisions on the strength of scientific evidence and standards of practice. It should also take into account whether including a particular drug in the formulary (or in a particular tier in the formulary) has therapeutic value in terms of safety and efficacy.

Formulary Categories and Classes

In developing a formulary, drugs are grouped into categories and classes of drugs that work in a similar way or are used to treat the same condition. MMA required CMS to request the United States Pharmacopeia (USP) to develop a list of categories and classes that plans may use and to periodically revise such classification as appropriate. A plan's formulary must include at least two drugs in each category or class used to treat the same medical condition (unless only one drug is available in the category or class, or two drugs are available but one drug is clinically superior). The two-drug requirement must be met through the provision of two chemically distinct drugs. (Plans cannot meet the requirement by including only two dosage forms or strengths of the same drug or a brand name and its generic equivalent.)

Six Classes of Clinical Concern

In general, drug plans are required to operate formularies that cover at least two drugs in each drug class. However, a higher standard of coverage has been established for six specific classes. CMS has required Part D plans to cover all, or substantially all, of the drugs in the following six drug categories: immunosuppressant, antidepressant, antipsychotic, anticonvulsant, antiretroviral, and antineoplastic. CMS instituted this policy to mitigate the risks and complications associated with a possible interruption of therapy for vulnerable populations. Plan sponsors cannot implement prior authorization or step therapy requirements (see "Utilization Management") that are intended to steer beneficiaries to preferred alternatives within these classes for beneficiaries currently taking a drug.[23]

Congress required in MIPPA that beginning in plan year 2010, CMS identify classes and categories of drugs that should be covered entirely by Part D plans to ensure that beneficiaries have access to certain life-saving therapies and to a wide variety of therapy options for certain conditions such as cancer (which may be different from the six classes currently required by CMS). PDP sponsors will be required to include all covered Part D drugs in the categories and classes identified. CMS issued an interim final rule effective January 16, 2009, that will allow the agency to consider adding these protected classes of drugs to the Part D program.[24]

Vaccines

Starting in 2008, Medicare drug plans must include all commercially available vaccines on their drug formularies (except for vaccines that are covered under Part B). TRHCA modified the definition of a Part D drug to include "for [Part D] vaccines administered on or after January 1, 2008, its administration." Consequently, beginning in 2008, Part D plans (rather than Part B) are required to cover the costs for the administration of Part D-covered vaccines as well as the vaccine itself.

Formulary Changes in a Plan Year

Plans are allowed to change some of the drugs they cover during the year. MMA provided that if plans remove drugs from their formularies during the year (or change their preferred or tiered status), they are required to provide notice on a timely basis to CMS, affected enrollees, physicians, pharmacies, and pharmacists. Changes to formularies may be made in the following circumstances:

- Plans can expand formularies by adding drugs, lowering the tier of a drug (thereby reducing copayments or coinsurance), or deleting utilization management requirements.
- Plans may not change therapeutic categories and classes during a year except to account for new therapeutic uses and newly approved Part D drugs.
- Plans can make formulary maintenance changes after March 1, such as replacing a brand-name drug with a new generic drug or modifying formularies as a result of new information on safety or effectiveness. These changes require CMS approval and 60 days' notice to appropriate parties.
- Plans can only remove drugs from a formulary, move covered drugs to a less-preferred tier status, or add utilization management requirements in accordance with approved procedures and after 60 days' notice to appropriate parties.[25] *Plans should make such changes*

only if enrollees currently taking the affected drugs are exempt from the formulary change for the remainder of the plan year.

Plans are not required to obtain CMS approval or give 60 days' notice when removing formulary drugs that have been withdrawn from the market by either the FDA or a product manufacturer.

Transition Policies
CMS established transition standards to ensure that new plan enrollees do not abruptly lose coverage for their drugs—for example, if a plan does not cover a drug a beneficiary is currently using. In such cases, a beneficiary can request that his or her physician check to see if the prescription can be switched to a similar drug that is on the plan's formulary, or if the physician determines that the specific drug is medically necessary, the doctor can request that the plan make an exception to its policy.

Plans are required to provide a temporary supply anytime within the first 90 days of a beneficiary's enrollment in a plan. The supply must be for 30 days (unless the prescription is written for less than 30 days) for any non-formulary drug. The requirement also applies to drugs that are on a plan's formulary but that require prior authorization or step therapy.

Utilization Management

Sponsors can lower their drug spending by applying various utilization management (UM) restrictions to drugs on their formularies. Sponsors must establish a reasonable and appropriate drug utilization management program that (1) includes incentives to reduce costs when medically appropriate and (2) maintains policies and systems to assist in preventing over-utilization and under-utilization of prescribed medications. Since 2006, the trend annually among plans has been to impose higher cost-sharing and utilization management controls to address the high costs of drugs.

Tiered Formularies
For drugs included on the formulary, sponsors may assign drugs to tiers that correspond to different levels of cost sharing. In general, this type of structure encourages the use of generic medications by putting them on a cost-sharing tier that requires the lowest out-of-pocket costs for beneficiaries and

discourages the use of expensive drugs by putting them on tiers that require higher out-of-pocket spending. Plans have flexibility in how the tiers are structured, and different plans may place the same drug in different tiers; drugs in the parallel tiers may differ in cost-sharing requirements. To illustrate, a four-tier formulary may be structured so that Tier 1 includes low cost generics, Tier 2 includes medium-cost preferred brand-name drugs,[26] Tier 3 contains higher cost non-preferred brand names, and very expensive or rare drugs are placed in Tier 4 (the "specialty tier").

Part D plans are permitted to use a specialty tier for expensive products (e.g., unique drugs and biologics). In this tier, there is no limit on cost-sharing and beneficiaries cannot appeal cost sharing for specialty tier drugs as they can for drugs in other tiers. Plans typically charge a percentage of the cost in the specialty tier. To ensure that the plan does not substantially discourage enrollment by specific patient populations, CMS will approve specialty tiers only under the following conditions: (1) there is only one specialty tier exempt from cost-sharing exceptions; (2) cost-sharing is limited to 25% in the initial coverage range;[27] and (3) only drugs with negotiated prices exceeding a threshold may be placed in the tier ($600 a month in 2009).

A recent study found that the median cost share for generics in a PDP increased to $7 for a month's supply of a drug in 2009, up from the $5 it had been for previous years of the Part D benefit.[28] Median cost sharing for preferred drugs in PDPs rose from $28 in 2006 to $38 in 2009; for non-preferred drugs over that same time period, it rose from $55 to $75. Medicare Advantage plans have seen fewer increases.

The percentage of PDPs that include a specialty tier has remained the same from 2006 to 2009, 82%, while the percentage of MA-PDs with such a tier has increased from 69% in 2006 to 97% in 2009. Median cost sharing in this specialty tier has risen for both PDPs and MA-PDs, from 25% of the drug cost in 2006 to 33% in 2009.

Other Drug Utilization Controls

These types of restrictions can include (1) prior authorization, in which the beneficiary, with assistance of the prescribing physician, must obtain the plan's approval before it will cover a particular drug; (2) step therapy, which means that a beneficiary must first try a generic or less-expensive drug to see if it works as well as the one prescribed; and (3) quantity limits, which limit the supply of drugs to the dosage or quantity it regards as normal to treat the condition, in order to reduce the likelihood of waste (e.g., the drug was not effective or had intolerable side-effects). For any of these utilization controls to be waived, a beneficiary's doctor needs to provide a statement indicating that the prescribed drug and dosage are medically necessary and to provide a rationale why the restriction is not appropriate.

PDPs are increasing their use of utilization management.[29] The share of formulary drugs subject to UM tools increased from 18% of listed drugs in 2007 to 26% in 2009 (number does not include tiering). Of the different types of UM tools, prior authorization increased from 8% to 12%, quantity limits from 12% to 16%, and step therapy from 1% to 3%.

Medication Therapy Management

Each Part D Sponsor is required to incorporate a Medication Therapy Management Program (MTMP) into its plan's benefit structure, and each year, sponsors are to submit a description of its MTMP to CMS for review and approval. A CMS-approved MTMP is one of several required elements in the development of sponsors' bids for the upcoming contract year.

The MTMPs are to target enrollees who have chronic diseases, are taking multiple Part D drugs, and are likely to incur annual costs for covered drugs that exceed a level specified by the Secretary ($4,000 in 2009 and $3,000 in 2010). Beneficiaries enrolled in a MTMP cannot be disenrolled later in the year, even if they no longer meet one of the eligibility criteria. Plans are to provide interventions for beneficiaries meeting all of the criteria regardless of the setting.

An approved MTMP must (1) ensure optimum therapeutic outcomes for targeted beneficiaries through improved medication use; (2) reduce the risk of adverse events for targeted beneficiaries; (3) be developed in cooperation with licensed and practicing pharmacists and physicians; (4) be coordinated with any care management plan established for a targeted individual under a chronic care improvement program; and (5) describe the resources and time required to implement the program if using outside personnel and establish the fees for pharmacists or others. The MTMP may be furnished by pharmacists or other qualified providers.

COVERAGE DETERMINATIONS, APPEALS, AND GRIEVANCES

As a beneficiary protection, Part D plans are required to have procedures in place for making timely coverage determinations, for handling appeals of coverage determinations, and for handling grievances. Beneficiaries can use the coverage determination and appeals process to challenge a utilization management restriction on a drug on the sponsor's formulary or to request coverage for a Part D drug that is not on the sponsor's formulary. The Medicare Part D program adapted many of the existing rules for grievance and appeals that apply to Medicare Advantage plans to prescription drug coverage.

CMS established priority levels for coverage determinations and appeal requests as either standard or expedited. Prescribing physicians may initiate coverage determinations and expedited redeterminations on behalf of a beneficiary without permission from the beneficiary, but to initiate a standard appeal on a beneficiary's behalf, the physician must have completed an appointment of representative form. Plans must ensure that all enrollees receive written information about these procedures.

Coverage Determination

A coverage determination is any decision (either an approval or denial) made by the plan sponsor with regard to covered benefits. Examples of coverage determinations include (1) a decision about whether to provide or pay for a Part D drug that the enrollee believes may be covered;[30] (2) a decision concerning a tiering exceptions request;[31] 3) a decision concerning a formulary exceptions request;[32] (4) a decision regarding the amount of cost-sharing; or (5) a decision on whether an enrollee has satisfied a prior authorization or other utilization management requirement.

A request for a coverage determination may be filed by the enrollee, the enrollee's appointed representative, or the enrollee's physician. The sponsor must notify the enrollee of its determinations within 72 hours of receipt of the request (or, in the case of an exceptions request, receipt of the physician's supporting statement). Plans must respond to a standard appeal within seven days. An enrollee can request an expedited decision; if the plan approves the request, it must make the determination within 24 hours. If the sponsor fails to notify the beneficiary of its decision within the established time frames, the decision is deemed an automatic denial, at which point the sponsor must forward the case to the independent review entity, the second level of appeal.

Appeals

If the plan sponsor's coverage determination is unfavorable to the enrollee, it must provide the enrollee with a written denial notice that includes information on appeals rights. An appeal is a request to have further review of a coverage determination.[33] There are five levels of appeals.

Redetermination

The first level of appeal is a *redetermination* by the plan. An enrollee, or an appointed representative, may request a standard or an expedited redetermination with respect to covered drug benefits or payments.

To request a redetermination, an individuals should write a letter to his/her plan asking for a redetermination of the decision not to cover a drug (or charge a higher level of cost-sharing). The letter should include the name of the drug that has been denied coverage, the reason for the denial, and reasons why the drug should be covered. The request should generally be filed within 60 days of the unfavorable coverage determination. The sponsor must provide the enrollee or prescribing physician with a reasonable opportunity to present evidence and the redetermination must be made by a person not involved in the original coverage determination.[34] Enrollees are to be notified of the results within seven days in the case of standard redetermination or within 72 hours for an expedited request.

Reconsideration by an Independent Review Entity

At the second level of appeal, an enrollee dissatisfied with a redetermination has a right to *reconsideration* by an independent review entity (IRE) that contracts with CMS for this purpose. An enrollee or an enrollee's appointed representative may request a standard or expedited reconsideration. The request must be made within 60 days of the redetermination. An enrollee's prescribing physician may not request a reconsideration on an enrollee's behalf unless the enrollee's physician is also the enrollee's appointed representative; however, the IRE must solicit the views of the prescribing physician. It is required to make a decision within seven days for a standard reconsideration and 72 hours for an expedited reconsideration.

Additional Levels of Appeal

If the above appeals result in decisions unfavorable to the enrollee, several additional levels of review may be pursued.

At the third level of appeal, an enrollee or the appointed representative may request a hearing with an *administrative law judge* (ALJ). An enrollee's prescribing physician may not request a hearing by an ALJ on an enrollee's behalf unless the enrollee's physician is also the enrollee's appointed representative. The request must be made within 60 days of the IRE decision letter. To qualify for an ALJ hearing, the projected value of denied coverage must meet a minimum dollar amount ($120 in 2009). No time frames are specified for ALJ action.

The fourth level of appeal is the *Medicare Appeals Council (MAC)*. A beneficiary or the appointed representative may request a review by the MAC within 60 days of the ALJ decision. The MAC may grant or deny the request for review. If it grants the request, it may issue a final decision or dismissal, or remand the case to the ALJ with instructions on how to proceed with the case. No times frames are specified for a MAC review.

The final appeal level is a *federal district court*. A beneficiary or the appointed representative may request a review by a federal court within 60 days of the MAC decision notice. To receive a review by the court, the projected value of denied coverage must meet a minimum dollar amount ($1,220 in 2009).

Grievances

Grievances are complaints or disputes other than those involving coverage determinations. Grievances may include such things as complaints about the plan's customer service hours of operation, time to obtain a prescription, or pharmacy charges. A grievance may also include a complaint that the Part D plan refused to expedite a coverage determination or redetermination. A beneficiary with a grievance should file the complaint within 60 days of the event. The plan sponsor must respond in a timely manner.

PART D PLANS: PAYMENT AND PARTICIPATION

Medicare Part D participants must obtain coverage through a private insurer, or other entity, that contracts with Medicare (a plan sponsor). As previously described, beneficiaries may select either a stand-alone prescription drug plan or a Medicare Advantage plan that includes prescription drug coverage along with other Medicare services.[35]

PDPs are required to be available regionwide within 1 of 34 Medicare-designated PDP regions in the United States. MA-PDs are generally local, operating on a countywide basis; however, regionwide MA-PDs are available in 22 of the 26 MA regions. A PDP sponsor may offer a PDP in more than one region, including all PDP regions; however, the sponsor must submit separate bids for its coverage in each region of its service area.[36]

Medicare's payments to plans are determined through a competitive bidding process, and enrollee premiums are tied to plan bids. Plans bear some risk for their enrollees' drug spending.

Approval of PDP Plans

Each year, CMS issues a call letter to sponsors planning to offer PDP and/or MA plans in the coming year. The 2009 call letter, issued in March 2008, combined contracting guidance for both programs.[37]

Potential PDP and MA sponsors are required to submit bids by the first Monday in June of the year prior to the plan benefit year. The following information must be included with the bid: (1) coverage to be provided; (2) actuarial value of qualified prescription drug coverage in the region for a beneficiary with a national average risk profile; (3) information on the bid, including the basis for the actuarial value, the portion of the bid attributable to basic coverage and, if applicable, the portion attributable to enhanced coverage, and assumptions regarding the reinsurance subsidy; and (4) service area. The bid also includes costs (including administrative costs and return on investment/profit) for which the plan is responsible. The bid must exclude costs paid by enrollees, payments expected to be made by CMS for reinsurance, and any other costs for which the sponsor is not responsible.

CMS reviews the information to conduct negotiations with the sponsors regarding the terms and conditions of the proposed bid and benefit plan and determines whether to approve the plan sponsor's bid submission. MMA specified that the Secretary's negotiating authority is similar to the authority the Director of the Office of Personnel Management has with respect to Federal Employees Health Benefits (FEHB) plans. However, the law specifically states that the Secretary may not interfere with the negotiations between drug manufacturers and pharmacies and PDP sponsors. Further, the Secretary may not require a particular formulary or institute a price structure for the reimbursement of covered Part D drugs. This is known as the "non-interference provision."[38]

CMS can approve a plan only if certain requirements are met. For example, CMS must determine that the plan and the sponsor meet requirements relating to actuarial determinations and beneficiary protections. Further, the plan is not to be designed in a way (including any formulary and tiered formulary structure) that would be likely to discourage enrollment by certain beneficiaries.

Once their bids have been approved, PDP sponsors enter into 12-month contracts with CMS. The contract may cover more than one Part D plan. Under the terms of the contract, the sponsor agrees to comply with Part D requirements and have satisfactory administrative and management arrangements.

Plan Availability

In 2007 and 2008, most beneficiaries were able to choose from 50 to 60 PDPs options. However, in 2009, the total number of PDPs available in each region declined to a median of 49 (1,689 total number of PDPs in 2009 compared with 1,824 in 2008).[39] (See Figure 2.). The decline is due to organizational mergers and acquisitions as well as withdrawals of certain benefit designs. For example, UnitedHealthcare and PaciCare merged in 2006 and reduced the number of combined plans over a three-year period. Additionally, several organizations—including Sterling, Longs Drug Stores, and Coventry—withdrew PDPs from the market that covered generic drugs for beneficiaries whose spending had reached the coverage gap.

In 2006 and 2007, Part D enrollment in PDPs was concentrated among a relatively small number of sponsors, with two organizations, UHC-PacifiCare and Humana, capturing nearly half of all Part D PDP enrollees. In 2008, these companies were still dominant, but their market shares declined to a combined 41% of the 17.4 million members in the PDP market because of reassignments of LIS enrollees to lower-premium plans. The third largest PDP sponsor in 2008, Universal American, accounted for 11% of enrollment. In 2008, 16 organizations that offered one or more PDPs in each of the 34 regions continued to account for 86% of PDP enrollment.

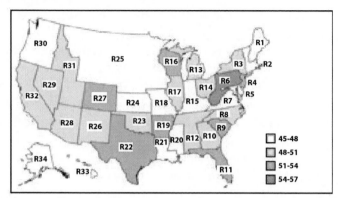

Source: Kaiser Medicare Health and Prescription Drug Plan Tracker, data from
Mathematica Policy Research analysis of CMS Prescription Drug Plan Landscape
file.

Figure 2. Prescription Drug Plans Available by Region, 2009

The number of MA-PDs offered in 2009 increased to 2,039 plans from
1,932 in 2008.[40] For MA-PDs, the same two organizations that had the largest
PDP membership, United Healthcare and Humana, also had the greatest
market shares of enrollment in MA plans that offer drug benefits, with United
Healthcare accounting for 17% and Humana for 15% of the 8.6 million
members in MA-PDs in 2008 (the same percentage as 2007).

Availability of Low-Income Plans

A Part D plan qualifies as a benchmark plan if it offers basic Part D
coverage with premiums equal to or lower than the regional low-income
premium subsidy amount. The regional low-income benchmark premium
amount, calculated annually, is the weighted average of all premiums in each
of the 34 prescription drug plan regions for basic prescription drug coverage,
or the actuarial value of basic prescription drug coverage for plans that offer
enhanced coverage options, or for Medicare Advantage Prescription Drug
plans (MA-PD), the portion of the premium attributable to basic prescription
drug benefits.

As a result of annual changes in the regional benchmarks and changes in
Part D plan offerings, the overall number of LIS benchmark plans has declined
from 483 plans (26% of all plans offered) in 2007 to 308 plans (18%) in
2009.[41] LIS beneficiaries who were enrolled in a benchmark plan that no

longer qualified in 2009 were either auto-enrolled in a new plan or needed to make a new plan selection in order to avoid paying premiums and other cost-sharing requirements. See Figure 3, "Premium Subsidies for Low-Income Populations," and "LIS Enrollment."

Plan Payments

For each Medicare enrollee in a plan (either stand-alone PDP or MA-PD), Medicare provides plans with a subsidy that averages 74.5% of standard coverage. The average subsidy takes two forms: *direct subsidy payments* and *reinsurance payments*. Medicare also establishes *risk corridors* to limit a plan's overall losses or profits. In addition, Medicare pays plans that enroll low-income beneficiaries most of their enrollees' cost sharing and premiums. Although plans receive essentially the same level of direct subsidy per enrollee (modified by risk adjusters), the level of subsidies granted through the other mechanisms differs substantially from plan to plan.

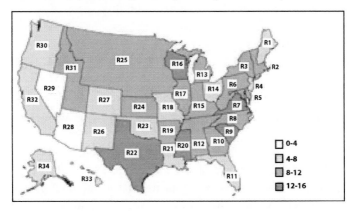

Source: Kaiser Medicare Health and Prescription Drug Plan Tracker, data from Mathematica Policy Research analysis of CMS Prescription Drug Plan Landscape file.

Notes:

- Refers to plans that have no additional premium when the full low-income subsidy is applied. These plans are eligible for auto-enrollment of dual eligibles and facilitated enrollment of those found eligible for low-income subsidies.
- Two LIS benchmark plans are available in Arizona (R28) and one in Nevada (R29).

Figure 3. Low-Income Subsidy Eligible Prescription Drug Plans, 2009 by Prescription Drug Plan Region

Direct Subsidies

Medicare makes monthly prospective payments to plans for each Part D enrollee. The payment is based on the nationwide average of plan bids for provision of basic drug coverage,[42] weighted by the plan's share of total enrollment.[43] (The national average monthly bid amount was $84.33 for plan year 2009.)[44] This amount is then risk-adjusted to take into account the health status of beneficiaries expected to enroll—plans with sicker enrollees receive a higher subsidy. The subsidy is further adjusted to cover expected additional costs associated with low-income enrollees (the low-income subsidy). Lastly, the payment amount is reduced by the base beneficiary premium for the plan.[45] (See "Premiums.")

Reinsurance Subsidies

As previously noted, in a standard plan design, Part D plans pay all drug costs above the catastrophic threshold ($6,154 in 2009) except for nominal beneficiary cost sharing. Medicare subsidizes 80% of the plans' costs for catastrophic coverage. Payments are made on a monthly basis during the year based on either estimated or incurred costs, with final reconciliation made after the close of the year.

Risk Corridor Payments

MMA established risk corridors to limit plans' overall risks or profits under the new program. Under risk corridors, Medicare limits a plan's potential losses, or gains, by financing some of the higher than expected costs, or recouping excessive profits.

Risk corridors are defined as specified percentages above and below a target amount and are set separately for each plan. The target amount is based on the total risk-adjusted subsidy payments paid to the plan plus beneficiary premiums, reduced by the administrative expenses assumed in the bid. The target amount is then compared to the plan's actual allowable costs.[46] If actual costs exceed the target amount, Medicare reimburses plans for a portion of their losses, and if costs are lower than the target, the sponsor may owe money to CMS.

Over time, as more experience has been gained with the program, the risk corridors have widened, thereby increasing the insurance risk borne by the plans. From 2008 to2011, drug plans bear all gains and losses that fall within 5% of their expected costs, compared with 2.5% in 2006 and 2007 (see Table 8). Beginning in 2012, CMS may widen the risk corridors further.

Table 8. Plan Liability Under Risk Corridor Provisions

Risk Corridor	Plan Liability for Costs Above and Below Target
2006-2007	
Costs below 95% of target	80% refund
Costs between 95% and 97.5% of target	75% refund
Costs between 97.5% and 102.5% of target	Full risk
Costs between 102.5% and 105% of target	Risk for 25% of amount
Costs over 105% of target	Risk for 20% of amount
2008-2011	
Costs below 90% of target	80% refund
Costs between 90% and 95% of target	50% refund
Costs between 95% and 105% of target	Full risk
Costs between 105% and 110% of target	Risk for 50% of amount
Costs over 110% of target	Risk for 20% of amount

Reconciliation

Following the close of the calendar year, CMS makes retroactive adjustments to the direct subsidy payments made to plans to reflect actual plan experience. To illustrate, the direct subsidy payments are adjusted based on updated data about actual beneficiary health status and enrollment. Additionally, prospective payments for reinsurance and low-income subsidy payments are compared to actual incurred costs, net of any direct or indirect remuneration (including discounts, chargebacks or rebates), and other related data, and appropriate adjustments are made to the plan payments. Finally, any necessary adjustments are made to reflect risk sharing under the risk corridor provisions.

In October 2007, CMS announced that it would collect $4 billion from Part D drug plan sponsors for the 2006 plan year because actual drug costs for almost all Part D plans were lower than the costs estimated in their 2006 bids. The 2007 bid submissions, which reflected the actual 2006 Part D program experience, were significantly lower than those submitted in 2006. Part D drug plan sponsors will return a net $18 million to CMS as part of the 2007 reconciliation process.[47] Not all insurers owed money back to the government, and some received additional payments because of higher than expected costs.

ENROLLMENT IN PART D

Enrollment Periods

A beneficiary who is signing up for Medicare Part D for the first time may do so in one of three different enrollment periods, depending on the individual's circumstances:

- Initial Enrollment Period for Part D.
- Annual Open Enrollment Period (or Annual Coordinated Election Period, AEP).
- Special Enrollment Periods (SEP).

Initial Enrollment Period

The initial enrollment period is the time during which an individual is first eligible to enroll in a Part D plan. Beneficiaries not yet enrolled in Medicare who have no other "creditable" coverage may join a drug plan at any time during their seven-month initial Medicare enrollment period. Creditable coverage is prescription drug coverage that is expected to cover at least as much as Medicare's standard prescription drug coverage.[48] This initial enrollment period is the same as that applicable for Medicare Part B. Coverage for these individuals begins on the first day of the month following the month of enrollment, but no earlier than the first month they are entitled to Medicare.

Annual Open Enrollment Period

In general, an individual who does not enroll during his or her initial enrollment period may enroll only during the annual open enrollment period, which occurs from November 15 to December 31 each year. Coverage begins the following January 1. Beneficiaries already enrolled in a Part D plan may change their plans during the annual open enrollment period.

Beneficiaries may wish to change PDP plans for a variety of reasons, including changes in their health and prescription drug needs or modifications by their plans. Generally, sponsors make changes to benefits offered by their plans effective at the beginning of each benefit year. After the opportunity to change plans during the AEP, most beneficiaries enrolled in Part D plans are locked into their plans for the benefit year.

Special Enrollment Periods

There are a few additional, limited occasions when an individual may enroll in or disenroll from a Part D plan or switch from one Part D plan to another, called special enrollment periods (SEPs). For example, SEPs are allowed for individuals who (1) move to a new geographic area, (2) involuntarily lose creditable coverage, (3) receive inadequate information on creditable coverage status, (4) are subject to a federal error, or (5) are enrolled in a PDP that has failed or been terminated.

Late Enrollment Penalty

The late enrollment penalty is assessed on persons who go for 63 days or longer after the close of their initial Part D enrollment period without creditable coverage and subsequently enroll in Part D. The penalty is intended to encourage all persons who do not have creditable coverage to enroll to prevent adverse selection. Adverse selection occurs when only those persons who think they need the benefit actually enroll in the program. When this happens, per capita costs can be driven up, thereby causing more persons (presumably the healthier, less costly ones) to drop out of the program. Over time, as more persons drop out, program costs could become prohibitive.

The penalty is based on the number of months an individual does not have creditable coverage.[49] For 2009, the penalty is based on 1% per month without creditable coverage of the 2009 national base premium ($30.36). As an example, if a beneficiary were eligible for Part D in June 2006, 31 months from January 2009, the individual would owe $9.41 per month more than if he or she had signed up in June 2006. The penalty would be applied permanently. For beneficiaries whose premium is withheld from Social Security benefits, the Social Security Administration increases the withhold amount by the amount of the penalty. For plan members in direct-bill status, the Part D plan sponsor is required to bill the beneficiary for the penalty at the same time that it bills for his or her Part D plan premium; the beneficiary may pay the penalty on a monthly basis or any other billing cycles offered by the plan. Dual-eligible beneficiaries or individuals who have qualified for the LIS program are not subject to the late enrollment penalty.

Plan Selection

Plans can make a number of changes to their benefit structures from one year to the next, including changing drugs included in the plan's formulary and/or changing the required cost-sharing charges for certain drugs. CMS requires that sponsors mail enrollees an Annual Notice of Change (ANOC) for receipt by October 31. This document describes modifications to the plan's premium, drug coverage, cost sharing, and other features for the next benefit year. This schedule provides beneficiaries with at least two weeks to review the ANOC prior to November 15, the first day plans can accept AEP enrollments.

In addition, sponsors are required to send beneficiaries other enrollment-related materials and information such as the Evidence of Coverage, a Summary of Benefits, a document describing the formulary, the plan's general utilization management policies and procedures, and a chart of covered drugs that includes the drug's name, tier placement, and any utilization management restrictions.

Each year, Medicare beneficiaries should review the costs for their current drug and health plans, (if in MA) including premiums, co-pays, and deductibles, and compare the cost and coverage to other plans in their area. Additionally, beneficiaries should consider in what tier the drugs are placed and what, if any, utilization management requirements the plan imposes for those drugs.

Information regarding and links to resources to compare the costs or benefits of Medicare prescription drug plans may be found on CMS's Open Enrollment Web page.[50] Additionally, beneficiaries and persons assisting them can help find a plan by using the Medicare drug plan finder.[51] After entering information on all the medications and dosages of each that the beneficiary currently takes, the plan finder shows the beneficiary the five plans in the area with the lowest total annual cost for that package of drugs.[52] The drug plan finder also provides an overall summary score of each drug plan's performance to make it easier to compare drug plans based on cost, quality, and performance ratings.[53]

Information on plan availability and characteristics can be obtained from a number of additional sources, including the Medicare toll-free information number (1-800-MEDICARE), State Health Insurance Assistance Programs (SHIPs),[54] and other local organizations.

Despite the potential for cost increases or changes in drug coverage from year to year, the vast majority of enrollees do not switch their drug plans.

According to MedPAC, since the program began in 2006, only about 6% of enrollees have switched plans voluntarily each year.[55]

Plan Marketing

Plan sponsors are required to ensure timely and accurate information in their marketing materials. In developing these materials for the 2009 open enrollment period, sponsors could choose to adopt CMS's model documents or to create non-model documents that contain CMS's required elements. Sponsors are required to submit all annual enrollment marketing materials to CMS for review prior to mailing to enrollees. In its 2009 call letter to plans,[56] CMS emphasized that as marketing is the primary means for organizations to attract people with Medicare to their products, providing accurate and reliable information is essential to helping inform beneficiaries of their choices. Therefore, organizations must provide training to marketing representatives on Medicare rules, regulations, and compliance-related information on the plan products they intend to sell.

On September 18, 2008, CMS published a final rule implementing certain MA and PDP marketing provisions in MIPPA.[57] Specifically, the rule prohibits plans from providing meals to prospective enrollees at promotional events; prohibits plans from cross-selling non-health care-related products during Medicare marketing activities; prohibits unsolicited contact with potential enrollees (e.g., door-to-door solicitation); restricts marketing activities in provider offices; requires that only state-licensed representatives conduct marketing activities; and defines certain terms related to marketing activities. The rule was effective September 18, 2009, and first applied to the 2009 benefit year marketing campaign.

A second rule, issued the same day,[58] addresses a variety of other MIPPA MA and Part D provisions and is subject to a public comment period. With regard to Part D and MA marketing, the rule, among other things, codifies the $15 limit on nominal gifts to prospective enrollees; codifies restrictions on co-branding; limits marketing appointments to the scope of health care-related products agreed upon by the beneficiary in advance; restricts agent/broker compensation arrangements to reduce financial incentives to move a beneficiary from one plan to another; and establishes requirements for agent/broker training and testing and the reporting of terminated agents/brokers.

Enrollment Process

Beneficiaries can join a Medicare drug plan in a variety of ways, including (1) filling out a paper application; (2) visiting the plan's website and enrolling online; (3) using the Medicare online enrollment center at www.medicare.gov;[59] (4) calling the company offering the drug plan; and (5) calling 1-800 Medicare. In general, a PDP sponsor cannot deny a valid enrollment request from any Part D-eligible individual residing in its service area.

An individual (or his/her legal representative) must complete an enrollment request, include all the information required to process the enrollment, and submit the request during a valid enrollment period. Upon receiving an enrollment request, a PDP sponsor must provide within 10 calendar days (1) a notice of acknowledgement of receipt of the beneficiary's application, (2) a request for more information in cases of incomplete applications, or (3) a notice that the application has been denied, along with an explanation of the reasons.

Prior to the effective date of enrollment, the PDP sponsor must provide the member with all the necessary information about being a Medicare member of the PDP, including the PDP rules and the member's rights and responsibilities. In addition, the PDP sponsor must provide the following: a copy of the completed enrollment form, if needed; a notice acknowledging receipt of the enrollment request providing the expected effective date of enrollment; and proof of health insurance coverage so that the beneficiary may begin using the plan services as of the effective date. For all enrollment requests, the PDP sponsor must submit the information necessary for CMS to add the beneficiary to its records as an enrollee of the PDP sponsor within seven calendar days of receipt of the compete enrollment request.[60]

LIS Enrollment

Special enrollment rules apply to low-income persons. Generally, there is a two-step process for low-income persons to gain Part D coverage. First, a determination must be made that they qualify for the assistance; second, they must enroll, or be enrolled, in a specific Part D plan. Most beneficiaries receiving low-income subsidies, including dual eligibles and nursing home residents, are permitted to switch plans throughout the year, unlike other Part

D enrollees who generally may switch plans only during the annual enrollment period at the end of the year.

Auto-Enrollment

Full-benefit dual-eligible individuals who have not elected a Part D plan are auto-enrolled into one by CMS.[61] First, CMS uses data provided by state Medicaid agencies to identify full-benefit dual-eligible individuals. Then, CMS identifies plan sponsors that offer at least one Part D plan in the region offering basic prescription drug coverage with a premium at or below the low-income premium subsidy amount in each PDP region. If more than one sponsor in a region meets the criteria, CMS auto-enrolls the beneficiary on a random basis among available PDP sponsors. CMS then identifies the individual plans offered by the sponsor that include basic drug coverage with premiums at or below the low-income premium subsidy amount. The beneficiary is then randomly assigned among the sponsor's plans meeting that criteria.

If the individual is not eligible to enroll in a PDP because he or she is enrolled in a Medicare Advantage plan (other than a MA-PFFS plan that does not offer Part D, or an MSA plan), CMS will direct the MA organizations to facilitate the enrollment of these individuals into an MA-PD plan offered by the same MA organization.

Some dual eligibles may find that they are auto-enrolled in a plan that may not best meet their needs. For this reason, they are able to change enrollment at any time, with the new coverage effective the following month. If an enrollee selects a plan with a premium above the low-income benchmark, he or she is required to pay the difference.

Facilitated Enrollment

CMS established a process labeled "facilitated enrollment" for enrollees in Medicare Savings programs (MSPs), SSI enrollees, and persons who applied for and were approved for low-income subsidy assistance. The basic features applicable to auto-enrollment for dual eligibles (i.e., identification of eligibility through SSA and/or Medicaid data, random assignment to plans with premiums below the low-income benchmark, and assignment of MA enrollees to the lowest-cost MA-PD plan offered by the MA organization) are the same for facilitated enrollment.

Reassignment of Certain LIS Beneficiaries

Because CMS subsidizes up to a specific premium amount for LIS-eligibles, and plan premiums may change each year, CMS may need to reassign some LIS recipients to different plans so they can continue to receive drug benefits with no or low Part D premiums. In 2009, 1.6 million low-income beneficiaries were reassigned to new plans.[62] Beneficiaries who changed plans after they were either auto-assigned or had their enrollment facilitated into a plan for the 2008 plan year did not have their selection changed by CMS for the 2009 plan year if their plan's premium was to go above the regional low-income subsidy. However, CMS notified these 620,000 beneficiaries that they needed to choose a new benchmark plan if they wanted to avoid paying a premium for Part D coverage in 2009.

PHARMACY ACCESS AND PAYMENT

PDP sponsors are required to establish a pharmacy network sufficient to ensure access to covered Part D drugs for all enrollees. They must demonstrate that they provide (1) convenient access to retail pharmacies for all enrollees, (2) adequate access to home infusion pharmacies for all enrollees, (3) convenient access to long-term care (LTC) pharmacies for residents of LTC facilities, and (4) access to Indian Health Service, Tribes, or Urban Indian Programs pharmacies operating in the sponsor's service area.[63]

Any Willing Pharmacy

Part D sponsors are required to permit any pharmacy willing to accept the sponsor's standard contracting terms and conditions to participate in the plan's network. CMS notes that the sponsors' standard terms and conditions may vary to accommodate geographic areas and types of pharmacies; however, all similarly situated pharmacies are to be offered the same standard terms and conditions. A Part D pharmacy may not require a network pharmacy to accept insurance risk as a condition of participation in its pharmacy network.

As a general rule, any pharmacy can participate in a Part D plan's network. However, plans may negotiate with a smaller number of pharmacies, or pharmacy chains, to become preferred pharmacies. In such instances, while beneficiaries have the option of going to any one of a large number of pharmacies in their community, by going to a preferred pharmacy, they would in general have lower cost sharing.

Retail Pharmacy Access

Part D sponsors must secure the participation in their pharmacy networks of a sufficient number of pharmacies that dispense drugs directly to patients (other than by mail order) to ensure convenient access to covered Part D drugs by plan enrollees. CMS defines convenient access as follows:

- In urban areas, at least 90% of Medicare beneficiaries in the Part D sponsor's service area on average live within 2 miles of a retail pharmacy participating in the sponsor's network.
- In suburban areas, at least 90% of Medicare beneficiaries in the sponsor's service area on average live within 5 miles of a retail pharmacy participating in the sponsor's network.
- In rural areas, at least 70% of Medicare beneficiaries in the sponsor's service area on average live within 15 miles of a retail pharmacy participating in the sponsor's network.

Mail-Order Pharmacy Access

The inclusion of mail order pharmacies in Part D plan networks is optional. However, such plans do not count toward meeting the retail pharmacy access requirements. Sponsors may designate a subset of formulary drugs (e.g., for particular tiers) for availability via network mail-order pharmacies. Plans that include mail-order pharmacies in their networks must allow enrollees to receive benefits, such as extended (e.g., 90-day) supply of covered drugs through a network retail pharmacy. However, beneficiaries making this choice could be subject to higher cost-sharing charges.

Long-Term Care Pharmacy Access

Part D sponsors must offer standard LTC pharmacy network contracts to all LTC pharmacies operating in their service area that request such contracts.

The pharmacy must be able to meet performance and service criteria specified by CMS as well as any standard terms and conditions established by the Part D sponsor for its network LTC pharmacies. Part D sponsors may not rely on out-of-network pharmacies to meet the LTC convenient access standards.

Out-of-Network Access

In general, a beneficiary must go to one of the pharmacies within one's network. However, Part D sponsors must ensure that their enrollees have adequate access to covered Part D drugs dispensed at out-of-network pharmacies when those enrollees cannot reasonably be expected to obtain covered Part D drugs at a network pharmacy. If a plan offers a mail-order option, a beneficiary can have a prescription filled at a local pharmacy or through mail order. Enrollees will likely be required to pay more for a covered Part D drug purchased out-of-network than one purchased at a network pharmacy.

Payments to Pharmacies

Plan sponsors negotiate with pharmacies to include a sufficient number and geographic distribution of pharmacies in their networks. The plan reimburses the pharmacy for the cost of the drug, plus a dispensing fee. Pharmacies set their own rates for dispensing drugs but may give the plan a discount on their usual rate.

MIPPA included provisions directed at prompt payments to pharmacies and related issues.[64] For plan years beginning on or after January 1, 2010, the negotiated contracts between pharmacies and PDP sponsors or MA-PD plans will be required to pay all "clean claims" submitted by pharmacies within the "applicable number of calendar days" after the date on which the claim is received.[65] This requirement will not apply to pharmacies that dispense drugs by mail order only or are located in, or contract with, a long-term care facility. If payment is not issued, mailed, or otherwise transmitted within the applicable number of calendar days after a clean claim is received, the PDP sponsor or MA-PD plan will be required to pay interest to the pharmacy that submitted the claim.

MIPPA also provided that for plan years beginning on or after January 1, 2010, contracts between PDP sponsors and pharmacies located in or contracting with long-term care facilities will be required to allow pharmacies between 30 and 90 days to submit claims for reimbursement. Additionally, for plan years beginning on or after January 1, 2009, contracts between pharmacies and PDP sponsors or MA-PD plans that use the cost of a drug as the standard for reimbursement of pharmacies are required to provide that the sponsor update the standard at least every seven days, to accurately reflect the market price of acquiring the drug.

EMPLOYER SUBSIDIES

MMA included provisions designed to encourage employers to continue to offer drug benefits to their Medicare-eligible retirees. Employers have a number of options in how they can provide prescription drug coverage to Medicare-eligible retirees.

Retiree Drug Subsidy

Employers and union groups that provide prescription drug insurance to their Medicare-eligible retired workers that is at least as generous as Part D coverage may apply to receive retiree drug subsidies (RDS) from Medicare. For a plan to participate, the sponsor's drug benefits must be at least actuarially equivalent to standard prescription drug coverage under Part D. Sponsors must submit applications to CMS no later than 90 days prior to the beginning of the plan year and receive approval in order to receive the subsidy.

In 2009, qualified sponsors receive a federal tax-free subsidy equal to 28% of the allowable gross retiree prescription drug costs over $295 through $6,000 for each beneficiary who is enrolled in the employment-based plan instead of Part D.[66] The dollar amounts are adjusted annually by the percentage increase in Medicare per capita prescription drug costs. In addition to encouraging employers to maintain drug coverage for their retirees, the RDS payments are generally less expensive for Medicare than enrolling these beneficiaries in a Part D drug plan. In 2008, the average RDS payment was about $560 per beneficiary.[67]

Subsidy payments are made on behalf of individuals who meet the criteria for a qualifying covered retiree. These standards require that the individual be entitled to Medicare benefits under Medicare Part A or enrolled in Medicare Part B, and live in the service area of a Medicare Part D plan; however, the individual cannot be enrolled in a Medicare Part D plan. The individual must also be a retired participant in the employer's qualified group health plan or the Medicare-enrolled spouse or dependent of the retired participant.

An individual retiree can elect to enroll in Part D, even if the former employer has elected to take the subsidy. (The employer would no then longer receive the subsidy payments for this individual.) However, any payments made by the employer plan would not count toward meeting the true out-of-pocket requirements.

In 2008, 6.7 million Medicare beneficiaries were enrolled in employer plans receiving the RDS; in 2009, 6.0 million receive drug coverage from these plans. As of October 2008, approximately 3,600 public and private employers have at least one approved application for the RDS.[68]

Alternatives

Employers or unions may select an alternative option (instead of taking the subsidy) with respect to Part D. These options include the following:

- They may elect to pay a portion of the Part D premiums for their eligible retirees.
- They may elect to set up their own separate plan that supplements, or "wraps around" Part D coverage.[69]
- Employers or unions may contract with a PDP or MA-PD to offer the standard Part D prescription drug benefits or enhanced benefits to its Medicare eligible retirees.
- Finally, they may become a Part D plan sponsor themselves for their retirees.

PROGRAM OVERSIGHT

The size, nature, and complexity of the Medicare Part D program put it at particular risk for fraud, waste, and abuse. For example, the Part D program involves particularly vulnerable beneficiaries, high-cost populations, and substantial control by plan sponsors, and creates a whole new category of payments and financial relationships. A variety of entities are involved in carrying out oversight activities to ensure compliance with program requirements and to identify potentially fraudulent activities.

CMS Oversight

CMS is responsible for preventing and detecting fraud and abuse in Medicare Part D and ensuring sponsors' compliance with applicable requirements. CMS conducts a wide variety of oversight activities, such as bid reviews, risk-adjustment validation reviews, financial and accounting reviews, program audits, and Part D LIS readiness audits.[70] Some of the management controls used in the routine operation of Medicare Part D have both a primary role in the administration of the benefit and a secondary role of fraud prevention and detection.

For each plan sponsor, CMS establishes a point of contact (account manager) for all communications with the plan. The account managers work with plans to resolve any plan problems, including compliance issues. In June of 2008, CMS reorganized the Center for Drug and Health Plan Choice to enhance focus on compliance and oversight activities, including consolidating Medicare Parts C and D data collection, measurement development, and performance analysis activities to facilitate a more data-driven approach to monitoring and oversight.

As part of its oversight strategy, CMS conducts routine *program audits* to ensure compliance with various program requirements, including enrollment and disenrollment, marketing and beneficiary information, grievances, pharmacy access, coordination of benefits, claims processing and payment, and grievances and coverage determinations.[71] CMS can also conduct separate, focused audits to confirm that a previously identified deficiency has been corrected or if there is an indication of noncompliance. These audits include a combination of desk and on-site activities.

In *financial audits*, CMS looks at the accuracy and validity of data reported by the plans. These audits, normally conducted after the payment reconciliation, may examine things such as possible overpayments to plans, misrepresentation of bids, underreporting of rebates, and inaccurate prescription drug event data. If financial audits identify problems, CMS will recalculate payment reconciliation for that sponsor and target the sponsor for a future audit. GAO reported that because of budget constraints, CMS completed only half the number of financial audits of 2006 plan year data that it intended to complete by October 2008.[72]

If egregious problems are identified, CMS actions can range from warning letters to civil monetary penalties or removal from the program, depending on the extent to which plans have violated Part D program requirements.

Oversight Responsibilities of Part D Sponsors

CMS requires plan sponsors to conduct activities to monitor and correct their own behavior, as well as the behavior of those they contract with. Part D sponsors are required by law to implement a comprehensive fraud and abuse program to detect, correct, and prevent fraud, waste, and abuse. Chapter 9 of CMS's *Prescription Drug Benefit Manual* provides both interpretive rules and guidelines for sponsors to follow in the development of this plan.[73] CMS is currently updating this chapter in response to recent regulatory changes and expects to issue the new version in late spring of 2009.[74]

Among other requirements, Part D sponsors are required to have and implement an effective compliance plan as a condition of participation in the Medicare program. Elements of an effective plan include written policies and procedures; a designated compliance officer and committee; training and education, effective lines of communication, well-publicized disciplinary guidelines, and internal monitoring and auditing; and prompt response to detected offences and development of corrective actions.

Beginning January 1, 2009, Part D sponsors are to provide fraud, waste, and abuse training and education to their first tier, downstream, and related entities.[75] This includes pharmacists, pharmacy clerks, and others who are employed by entities that plans contract with to provide the Medicare drug benefit.

Medicare Prescription Drug Integrity Contractors

CMS contracts with private firms, Medicare Prescription Drug Integrity Contractors (MEDICs), to perform a variety of fraud prevention detection activities. MEDIC responsibilities include conducting complaint investigations; performing data analysis; developing and referring cases to law enforcement, as well as supporting ongoing investigations; conducting audits; and beginning in September 2008, reviewing PDP and MA-PD fraud and abuse compliance programs. For example, a benefit integrity audit, also called a *targeted audit*, is performed if there is a concern that the activities of a sponsor could put the program and/or a beneficiary at risk.

MEDICs are also responsible for working with other entities to coordinate fraud prevention and detection efforts, including the Part D sponsors, other Medicare contractors, the HHS Office of Inspector General (OIG), the Department of Justice, and state agencies.

There are currently two MEDIC regions. The MEDIC North contractor is Electronic Data Systems Corporation, and the MEDIC South Contractor is Delmarva/Health Integrity.

ISSUES

The Medicare prescription drug program is now in its fourth year of operation. While early startup issues have generally been resolved, some issues remain and other issues are emerging. Additionally, initial reviews of the operations of the program have been completed and shed some light on areas where efficiencies may be realized, as well as areas where program vulnerabilities exist. Finally, discussions regarding the overall structure of the program benefits, costs to beneficiaries, and the pricing of and access to prescription drugs continue.

Beneficiary Costs

The basic structure of the Part D benefit, including the coverage gap and the ability of private health plans to affect access through deductibles, cost sharing, and drug formularies, may contribute to problems with affording prescription drugs, particularly for lower-income beneficiaries who do not qualify for the low-income subsidy. These features mean that out-of-pocket costs can vary considerably over the course of a year and depend on the specific drugs beneficiaries' physicians prescribe for them. It is possible that drug access problems for Medicare beneficiaries may grow in the future.

Premium Costs

More than 90% of beneficiaries would have experienced an increase in premiums between 2008 and 2009 if they did not change drug plans.[76] In their 2009 March report to Congress, MedPAC noted that if enrollees stayed in the same PDP, their premiums have risen by an average of $6 above the average 2008 level of $25 to nearly $31 per month, a 24% increase.

CMS attributed the hikes to rising drug costs, a change in how premium benchmarks are weighted for 2009, and plans' higher-than-expected costs for providing drug coverage above the catastrophic limit. In recent testimony, MedPAC Chairman Glenn Hackbarth suggested that the increases may have to do with pricing strategies to maximize market share, inadequate risk-adjustment, and monopolistic behavior by manufacturers of high-cost, single-source drugs.[77]

Coverage Gap

The number of PDPs offering drug coverage in the coverage gap continues to decline. An estimated 8.3 million Part D enrollees reached the coverage gap in 2007.[78] Approximately 2.9 million of those were not eligible for LIS or enrolled in a plan with gap coverage, and were therefore responsible for the full cost of their prescriptions. In 2009, only about 25% of PDPs and 51% of MA-PD plans offer some sort of gap coverage.[79]

Recent studies have found that some enrollees do not take needed medications when reaching the coverage gap. One study that looked at utilization of drugs in eight drug classes found that, on average, 15% of beneficiaries using drugs in these classes stopped taking them once they reached the gap.[80] According to findings from the Center for Studying Health System Change's 2007 Health Tracking Household Survey,[81] about 2.5 million Medicare beneficiaries went without at least one prescribed medication because of finances. Twenty-one percent of dual-eligible beneficiaries were also in this category, despite receipt of the low-income subsidy.

With many Part D enrollees at risk of forgoing needed medications in the coverage gap, or of incurring high out-of-pocket spending, concerns related to the coverage gap are likely to continue. Suggestions to address these problems have included proposals to simplify the benefit design by requiring that plans cover all generics, all brands, or no drugs in the coverage gap and clearly describe these definitions in the benefit descriptions. CBO has also proposed extending the benefit's initial 25% coinsurance rate up to the point at which the catastrophic threshold is reached. Implementing this option would increase total mandatory spending by an estimated $134 billion from 2010 through 2019.[82]

Utilization Controls

The trend annually among plans has been to impose higher cost sharing and utilization management controls to address the high cost of some drugs. For example, placing high-cost drugs in specialty tiers where cost sharing is set at a percentage of the cost of the drug can make these drugs unaffordable for some beneficiaries. There is concern that these kinds of structures pass additional costs to beneficiaries with the greatest health care needs. Additionally, although Medicare beneficiaries pay substantially more for specialty-tier drugs than for drugs on other tiers, Part D regulations preclude them from requesting an exception to reduce cost sharing for specialty drugs.

To illustrate, research conducted by Avalere Health and the American Cancer Society Cancer Action Network found that Medicare stand-alone PDPs have been increasingly shifting name-brand oral cancer drugs to higher formulary tiers over the past four years, meaning that each year consumers face higher cost sharing for these products.[83] In 2009, the large majority of PDPs placed name-brand oral oncology products on specialty tiers that require cost sharing of 26% to 35% for each prescription. Additionally, PDPs are increasing their use of prior authorization to control access to branded cancer drugs. The American Cancer Society is concerned that the shifts in drug coverage may limit access to treatment for people with cancer and reduce their treatment options.

One suggestion to help stem rising consumer costs associated with expensive specialty tier prescription drugs is to create a regulatory pathway for generic versions of biologic drugs and drive down costs through competition. Other suggestions are to limit the cost sharing for specialty tiers to 25% and to allow an exceptions process for specialty tiers.

There is also concern that plans have been given too much discretion in setting negotiated prices and thus may allow the inclusion of a wider range of therapies in the specialty tier (i.e., exceed the $600 threshold). Suggestions have included requiring plans to better define the way in which they calculate the threshold amount.

Program Costs

While Part D has increased medication access for Medicare beneficiaries, questions about cost continue to arise, and strategies to reduce and/or contain these costs are at the forefront of discussions related to Part D.

Part D Means-Testing

Most Part D enrollees pay a standard premium that is intended to cover about 25% of the program's average costs per capita. By comparison, Medicare's Part B charges progressively higher premiums for beneficiaries whose income exceeds certain levels. Means-testing Medicare Part D has been included in the President's 2010 budget as a cost-containment strategy, with estimated savings of $8.1 billion by 2019. The income levels and monthly adjusted premiums used to determine higher premiums for Part D would be the same as that applied to means-testing Part B. For 2009, that would mean that beneficiaries making at least $85,000 for an individual income tax return and $170,000 for a joint return would be charged additional premiums.[84] Proponents of this option maintain that it would offer budgetary savings but leave the majority of Part D enrollees unaffected. CBO estimates that fewer than 6% of Part D enrollees would face a higher premium in a given year, and all of those individuals would still be receiving subsidized coverage.[85]

Beneficiary advocacy groups maintain that the cost savings estimates are too high and are concerned about any additional economic pressures on retirees, especially in a difficult economy. Additionally it is possible that some higher income enrollees might react by opting out of the Part D program.[86]

Negotiation of Drug Prices

One of the most prominent issues relates to whether negotiation of drug prices should remain in the private sector or whether the federal government should be involved. Proponents of government involvement in negotiation of drug prices believe that the government could leverage its purchasing power to obtain lower drug prices. Some Members of Congress, contending that the combined purchasing power on behalf of all Medicare Part D beneficiaries could be used as leverage, have proposed amending the law to provide for the Secretary of HHS to negotiate directly with drug manufacturers. Opponents believe that market competition among private plans would result in lower overall drug prices, and that direct government negotiation could lead to a restriction of formulary choice and reduced funding for research and development. There is also some concern that pricing of medications for non-Medicare beneficiaries would be raised to offset the lower prices to Medicare.

CBO has concluded that while cost savings may be possible in selective instances, the impact of government negotiations would likely be limited.[87] Additionally, drug manufacturers could seek to limit the impact of the Secretary's actions by setting higher initial prices for their drugs to offset any potential price concessions from negotiations with the Secretary. The key factor in determining whether negotiations would lead to price reductions is the leverage that the Secretary would have to secure larger price concessions from drug manufacturers than competing PDPs currently obtain. When several drugs are available to treat the same medical condition, PDPs can secure rebates from selected drug manufacturers by giving their drugs preferred status within formularies. CBO stated that negotiation is likely to be effective only if it is accompanied by some source of pressure on drug manufacturers to secure price concessions.

Public Option

The rise in Part D premiums, the drop in the number of low cost options, and potentially discriminatory cost-sharing structures have led some to conclude that private markets without competition from a public health insurance plan option are not able to control costs and provide stability for beneficiaries.

With the creation of a publically administered prescription drug plan, seniors could chose between a government-operated plan that could negotiate directly with drug companies to lower medication prices. Proponents of such legislation maintain that this would create fair-market competition and lead to less costly drug choices for Medicare recipients. Opponents of this option believe that the competitive market approach is working well for beneficiaries and taxpayers and do not see a reason for the government to inject itself into the process.

Price Transparency

The Part D program relies on sponsors to generate prescription drug savings, in part, through their ability to negotiate price concessions such as rebates and discounts, with drug manufacturers and retail pharmacies. Sponsors must report the price concession amounts to CMS and pass some of these price concessions on to the beneficiaries. CMS uses the reported data to calculate final payments; however, much of the information submitted to CMS is protected from disclosure.

GAO has reported challenges in the oversight of federal prescription drug programs that rely on privately reported data.[88] CMS officials noted that variation in defining and reporting price concessions data, such as variation in how sponsors allocate manufacturer rebates between their Part D plans and other businesses, are likely to create oversight challenges. GAO identified CMS's actions to ensure that the price information Part D sponsors report to CMS include the aggregate price concessions that sponsors negotiate with PBMs and drug manufacturers as an area for congressional oversight.

A key question is where rebates to PDPs lie in the overall distribution of rebates and, consequently, how the net cost of drugs acquired by PDPs compares to the net cost other purchasers face. CBO has suggested that PDPs have secured rebates somewhat larger than the average rebates observed in commercial health plans.[89] An October 2007 report conducted by the Committee on Oversight and Government Reform concluded that Part D plans received low average rebates compared to Medicaid or the VA.

The lack of transparency in the actual net prices plan sponsors pay for drugs may result in overpayments to plans by Medicare. One option suggested by CBO is to require manufacturers of brand-name drugs to pay the federal government a rebate equaling 15% of the average manufacturer price. [90] Under this option, manufacturers would be required to participate in the rebate program in order for their drugs to be covered by parts B and D of Medicare, by Medicaid, and by the VA.

Classes of Clinical Concern

CMS has required Part D to cover all, or substantially all, of the drugs in six drug categories to ensure that beneficiaries have continued access to certain therapies for which restricted access could have serious clinical consequences. Additionally, MIPPA required the Secretary to identify categories and classes of drugs for which restricted assess to these drugs would have major or life-threatening consequences, and there is a significant need for individuals to have access to multiple drugs in this category.

There are concerns that if sponsors are required to offer all drugs in a category, there is little to no leverage for sponsors in negotiating with manufacturers and wholesalers to provide discounts. Therefore it may be difficult for sponsors to offer drugs at reduced prices (e.g., preferred drugs), thus resulting in potentially higher costs to Medicare and its beneficiaries. It is also possible that CMS's review could lead to additional drugs being added to those in the six classes already identified, thus resulting in potential additional increased costs to Medicare and its beneficiaries. A survey conducted by

Milliman estimates that the inclusion of all drugs in certain designated classes could cost the Medicare program as much as an additional $511 million per year.[91]

Marketing

In spite of recent changes in the law that place greater restrictions on marketing activities, marketing problems continue. For example, some beneficiaries have been pressured into buying Medicare insurance plans that they do not understand or want. In some cases, beneficiaries are sold Medicare Advantage plans without realizing that this means leaving traditional Medicare.[92] CMS's call letter for the 2010 plan year, issued March 30, 2009, also notes that in spite of actions over the last few years to strengthen marketing requirements and oversight, particularly of agent and broker conduct, "some of our contractors and related third-party entities attempt to find ways to circumvent our rules and guidelines."[93] The letter specifically warns against offering "exorbitant" fees to agents for making a referral and noted that in some instances referral fees exceeded the total compensation that can be paid to agents under Medicare rules.

As an example, in a February 19, 2009 letter, CMS notified the Tampa-based provider WellCare Health Plans Inc. that as of March 7, 2009, the company's Medicare enrollment and marketing activities would be suspended. Among the compliance problems cited was that WellCare engaged in activities that "misled and confused Medicare beneficiaries and misrepresented its organization." The company also engaged in unauthorized door-to-door solicitation and failed to establish and maintain a system for confirming that enrolled beneficiaries had, in fact, enrolled in its plan and understood the rules applicable to the plan. WellCare also failed to identify, monitor, and correct practices of agents who misrepresented its plans, including failing to discover forged applications through its own monitoring systems.

Part D related marketing activities will require continued monitoring and oversight to determine whether new laws and CMS requirements would result in fewer marketing abuses. However, in cases where the applicable requirements are not being adhered to, attention may need to be given to developing additional strategies to deter and/or stop inappropriate marketing activities.

Plan Selection and Enrollment

The structure of the Part D program, and the large number of plans in each region, can make a comparison of plans difficult. For example, beneficiaries must consider premiums, cost sharing, and costs covered in the coverage gap. They also must check whether the drugs they use will be covered by their plan and under what conditions. In spite of the many resources available to beneficiaries to assist them in selecting a plan, many observers have suggested that the range of plan options is confusing for some Medicare beneficiaries and that, as a result, beneficiaries may not enroll in the plans that best meet their needs.

Recent studies have also concluded that most beneficiaries do not have access to understandable information or effective assistance for making good decisions about their health care options. For example, a GAO study noted that the Annual Notice of Change (ANOC) contains language at too high a level for some beneficiaries and contained much needless and overly technical information.[94] GAO also noted that CMS did not take steps to formally evaluate this notice for the 2008 and 2009 enrollment periods for effectiveness in communicating plan changes.[95]

Additionally, a recent report found that in 2006, most of the seniors in the analysis did not choose the lowest-cost Part D plan available to them.[96] It is possible that beneficiaries chose a plan that contracts with a convenient pharmacy that may not be the lowest cost plan, that beneficiaries make their selections based on the nature of utilization restrictions, that they select a plan with a strong brand name, or are simply confused by the number and complexity of the plan offerings.

To make drug plan offerings more understandable and easier to compare, some have advocated for imposing standardization among plans to reduce variation (e.g., similar to Medigap plans) and/or limiting the number of Part D plans offered in each region. Additionally some, such as GAO, have suggested that CMS expand oversight to ensure that information provided to beneficiaries about their plan choices is accurate and understandable.

Appeals Process

There are concerns that the number of layers of the appeals and associated time delays can mean that beneficiaries may go without medically necessary drugs for an extended period. Additionally, the process can be confusing and information about the process may not always be readily available to beneficiaries when needed. Suggestions to help ensure timely access to non-formulary drugs or non-preferred drugs include requiring that information on the appeals process is provided at the pharmacy, and establishing a more efficient appeals process with fewer administrative burdens.

Low-Income Beneficiaries

The Medicare drug benefit offers substantial help to low-income Medicare beneficiaries, who generally have more medical and pharmaceutical needs than higher-income beneficiaries. Issues of concern with regard to the LIS program include lower than anticipated enrollment in LIS and the declining availability of LIS plans.

A continued interest will be the ability to identify and enroll persons eligible for the low-income subsidy who are not currently enrolled. Approximately one in five low-income Medicare beneficiaries estimated to be eligible for this assistance are not receiving it, and many individuals with low incomes do not qualify because their resources are just above the allowable threshold. In a September 2008 study,[97] GAO found that in 2006 and 2007, applicants denied the LIS often exceeded the asset threshold by a relatively small amount, and in both years more than one-quarter of these applicants exceeded the threshold by less than $5,000.

Additionally, the number of Medicare drug plans available to LIS recipients for no monthly premium has steadily declined since 2007. In 2009, LIS beneficiaries in most states have only a handful of PDPs available to them for no monthly premium, compared with the non-LIS beneficiaries who may have close to 50 plans to choose from. Although LIS beneficiaries have the right to switch plans at any time, those who choose to shop around are faced with increasingly limited options if they want to maintain their full premium subsidy.

The decline in the availability of LIS plans has led to the disruption in drug coverage for low-income Part D enrollees, affecting more than 1.0 million low-income beneficiaries between 2006 and 2007, 2.1 million between 2007 and 2008, and 1.6 million between 2008 and 2009. This does not include the LIS beneficiaries (over 600,000 in 2008) who switched out of the plan to which they were originally assigned and who needed to enroll in another plan to avoid paying premiums and cost sharing. Additionally, the random process for assigning low-income recipients to Part D plans has raised concerns because it does not take into account the specific drug needs of the individual and can possibly lead to negative consequences for enrollees' access to medications.

A number of potential solutions to address these problems have been promoted. One option would be for CMS to increase the pool of plans available to LIS recipients to include plans that offer enhanced benefits if their premiums are below the regional benchmarks. Additionally, Congress could review how the Part D low-income subsidy benchmark is calculated and whether a statutory change is needed to ensure that enough plans qualify each year to offer zero-premium coverage to low-income enrollees. An approach to ensure that LIS beneficiaries are enrolled in the best plans for them would be to adopt a more beneficiary-centered way to assign beneficiaries to plans based on their individual drug needs. Suggestions to address enrollment issues have also included permitting seniors to keep more of their assets and still qualify for the Medicare low-income assistance.

Adequacy of Oversight

Reports by OIG and GAO raise questions about the oversight of the Part D program by CMS and plan sponsors' compliance with fraud and abuse detection policies. Shortcomings identified include failures to conduct effective training and education for staff or implement procedures for effective internal monitoring and auditing. Additionally, there are concerns that Part D plans' fraud and abuse programs are designed largely to protect the plans themselves rather than the Medicare program or its beneficiaries

For example, a 2008 GAO report noted that "little is known about the extent to which Part D sponsors have implemented their fraud and abuse programs or the extent of CMS's oversight of Part D sponsors' programs." [98] CMS's oversight of the plans was primarily limited to the review and approval of sponsors' fraud and abuse program plans submitted as part of the plans' initial application for the program. The report also noted that CMS had not conducted its own audit of Part D plan fraud and abuse programs in 2007 and did not plan to conduct any in 2008. In response to the GAO report, CMS noted that it had relied on self-assessment by the sponsors because of a lack of adequate funding for adequate on-site fraud and abuse program audits.

Future discussions may focus on issues such as the adequacy of funding for Part D oversight (and funding for Medicare program oversight activities in general), the efficiency and effectiveness of current fraud and abuse detection activities, and identification and development of improved oversight methods and tools.

ACKNOWLEDGMENTS

Jennifer O'Sullivan made a significant contribution to this report.

End Notes

[1] The regulations governing the Part D program are set forth in 42 CFR Part 423—Voluntary Medicare Prescription Drug Benefit.

[2] 2009 Annual Report of the Boards of Trustees of the Federal Hospital Insurance and Federal Supplementary Medical Insurance Trust Funds, May 12, 2009, Table III.C17, p. 115.

[3] Medicare makes monthly prospective payments to Part D sponsors based on average plan bids that are adjusted for the expected case mix of enrollees in a particular plan. The new methodology would base the risk scores on the health status of individuals enrolled in Part D rather than on all those eligible for the benefit, starting in 2010. CMS published this policy in its April 6, 2009 release of the CY2010 "Medicare Advantage Capitation Rates and Medicare Advantage and Part D Payment Policies".

[4] The Medicare Savings program includes the Qualified Medicare Beneficiary program (QMB), Specified Low-Income Medicare Beneficiary program (SLMB), and Qualified Individual program (QI). These programs help Medicare beneficiaries of modest means pay all or some of Medicare's cost-sharing amounts (i.e., premiums, deductibles, and copayments). To qualify, an individual must be eligible for Medicare and must meet certain income limits which change annually.

[5] Supplemental Security Income (SSI) is a federal income supplement program funded by general tax revenues (not Social Security taxes). It is designed to help aged, blind, and disabled people who have little or no income, and it provides cash to meet basic needs for food, clothing, and shelter.

[6] Social Security benefits, Veterans benefits, public and private pensions, annuities, and in-kind support are counted as income.

[7] These resource limits include $1,500 per person for burial expenses.

[8] Social Security Administration's analysis of Medicare Database, February 1, 2008, cited in "Medicare Part D Low-Income Subsidy: SSA Continues to Approve Applicants, but Millions of Individuals Have Not Yet Applied," GAO-08-812T, May 22, 2008.

[9] Medicare Advantage plans are required to use 75% of the difference between the plan's benchmark payment and its bid for providing required Part A and Part B services (called the *Part C rebate*) to supplement its package of benefits or lower its premium. Many MA plans use some of their rebate dollars to enhance their Part D benefit or to reduce the portion of their plan premium associated with drug coverage.

[10] Also known as the "doughnut hole."

[11] Nominal cost sharing is defined as the greater of (1) a copayment of $2.40 in 2009 for a generic drug or preferred multiple source drug and $6.00 in 2009 for other drugs, or (2) 5% coinsurance.

[12] Medicare Payment Advisory Commission, "Report to Congress, Medicare Payment Policy," March 2009, Table 4-3.

[13] Ibid.

[14] Ibid.

[15] CMS, October 30, 2008, Medicare Prescription Drug Benefit Symposium, "Beneficiary Experience," http://www.cms.hhs.gov/PrescriptionDrugCovGenIn/08_PartDData.asp.

[16] Jack Hoadley et al., "Medicare Part D 2009 Data Spotlight: The Coverage Gap," Kaiser Family Foundation, November 2008.

[17] Initially, several sponsors offered full gap coverage but discontinued offering such coverage after experiencing significant adverse selection by high-cost enrollees.

[18] Part D sponsors are required to ensure that their network pharmacies inform enrollees of any price differential between a covered drug and the lowest-price generic version of the drug that is therapeutically equivalent, bioequivalent, on the plan's formulary, and available at that pharmacy.

[19] Some states offer payment assistance for drug plan premiums and/or other drug costs for individuals who have trouble affording their medication but do not qualify for LIS. For example, a state may offer assistance to individuals with incomes between 150% and 300% of the FPL. To learn which states offer this assistance and for details on the state programs, see http://www.medicare.gov/spap.asp.

[20] Many of the major drug manufacturers offer assistance programs for the drugs they manufacture. The value of the benefits received under these programs do not count toward true out-of-pocket expenses. To learn which manufacturers offer assistance, see http://www.medicare.gov/pap/index.asp.

[21] The law prohibits the Secretary from interfering with the negotiations between drug manufacturers and pharmacies and PDP sponsors. See "Approval of PDP Plans" for further detail.

[22] On January 12, 2009, CMS published a final rule (74 FR 1494) requiring Medicare Part D plan sponsors to use the amount paid to the pharmacy as the basis for determining cost sharing for beneficiaries and reporting a plan's drug costs to CMS. The changes must be implemented by the start of the 2010 plan year. Under current rules, Part D sponsors that contract with a PBM may report to CMS the amount paid to the PBM (the lock-in price) or the amount the PBM paid to the pharmacy (the pass-through price).

[23] For beneficiaries beginning treatment in these categories, such management techniques may be used for categories other than HIV/AIDS drugs.

[24] 74 *Federal Register* 2881. Although the rule is effective for the 2010 plan year, CMS indicated that it would not make any changes to the current policy for protected classes of drugs until the 2011 plan year because it had too little time to establish the review process for adding protected classes and creating exceptions to those requirements. The interim final rule also addresses a MIPPA-mandated change to the regulatory definition of "Part D drug," which expands the list of drug compendia CMS is to use to determine the medically accepted indications of anticancer therapies. It requires Part D sponsors to use the same definition for a "medically accepted indication" for anti-cancer drugs used for Medicare Part B, effective January 1, 2009.

[25] Plans may not remove covered Part D drugs from their formularies, or make any change in preferred or tiered cost-sharing status of a covered Part D drug, between the beginning of the annual coordinated election period and 60 days after the beginning of the contract year.

[26] Each plan negotiates the price of each drug with its manufacturer. If a plan obtains a good discount on one brand-name drug, but not on a competing drug used in treating the same condition, the plan may charge a lower co-pay for the former (preferred) drug and a higher co-pay for the latter (non-preferred).

[27] Sponsors may impose higher coinsurance in this tier to maintain actuarial equivalence in basic benefits (e.g., to offset a lower than standard deductible).

[28] Jack Hoadley et al., "Medicare Part D Benefit Designs and Formularies, 2006-2009," Presentation to MedPAC, December 5, 2008.

[29] Ibid.

[30] This includes a decision not to pay because the drug is not on the plan's formulary, the drug is determined not medically necessary, or the drug is furnished by an out-of-network pharmacy.

[31] MMA provided that if a Part D plan includes a tiered cost-sharing structure, a plan enrollee can request an exception to the structure. Under an exception, a non-preferred drug could be covered as a preferred drug if the prescribing physician determined that the preferred drug for treatment of the same condition would not be as effective for the individual, would have adverse effects for the individual, or both.

[32] MMA provided that a beneficiary enrolled in a Part D plan can appeal a determination not to provide coverage for a drug not on the plan's formulary. The appeal can only be made if the prescribing physician determines that all covered Part D drugs on any tier of the formulary for treatment of the same condition would not be as effective for the individual as the non-formulary drug, would have adverse effects for the individual, or both.

[33] Individuals can appeal coverage determinations related to formulary drugs and non-formulary drugs. They cannot appeal denial of coverage for excluded drugs.

[34] If the issue is the denial of coverage based on medical necessity, the redetermination must be made by a physician.

[35] The Part D sponsors are private entities licensed to offer health insurance under state law. Alternatively, they could meet solvency standards established by CMS for entities not licensed by the state.

[36] If two or more plans are not available in a region (one of which is a PDP), Medicare is required to contract with a non-risk "fallback" plan to serve beneficiaries in that area. Because of the large number of Part D plans participating in the program, CMS has not needed to solicit bids from fallback contractors.

[37] See http://www.cms.hhs.gov/PrescriptionDrugCovContra/Downloads/CallLetter.pdf. The 2010 call letter was issued March 30, 2009, and contains guidance to plans that will be submitting bids for the 2010 plan year; http://www.cms.hhs.gov/PrescriptionDrugCovContra/Downloads/2010CallLetter.pdf

[38] Social Security Act § 1860D-11(i).

[39] Medicare Payment Advisory Commission, "Report to Congress, Medicare Payment Policy," March 2009.

[40] Ibid.

[41] Laura Summer et al., "Medicare Part D 2009 Data Spotlight: Low-Income Subsidy Plan Availability," Kaiser Family Foundation, November 2008.

[42] The calculation of the national average monthly bid amount does not include bids submitted by Medical Savings Account (MSA) plans, MA private fee-for-service plans, specialized MA plans for special needs populations (SNP), Program of All-Inclusive Care for the Elderly (PACE) plans, or plans established through reasonable cost contracts.

[43] In 2006, the first year of Part D, there was no prior PDP enrollment information; therefore, each PDP plan was weighted equally (though MA-PD bids were enrollment-weighted if they had 2005 MA enrollment). Rather than immediately moving to full enrollment weighting in 2007, CMS provided for a phase-in under its demonstration authority. In 2007, 80% of the national monthly bid amount was based on the 2006 averaging methodology and 20% on the enrollment-weighted average. In 2008, 40% was based on the 2006 averaging methodology and 60% on the enrollment-weighted average. In 2009 and thereafter, the national bid amount is fully weighted by plan enrollment.

[44] The national average monthly bid amount was $80.43 for plan year 2007 and $80.52 for 2008.

[45] CMS takes plans' standardized bid amounts for basic benefits or the portion of plan bids attributable to basic coverage and calculates the average. From this nationwide average, plan enrollees must pay a base premium ($30.36 in 2009) plus any difference between their plan's bid and the nationwide average bid.

[46] Allowable costs include Part D drug costs minus the reinsurance subsidy and direct and indirect remuneration from drug manufacturers.

[47] For 2007, UHC-Pacificare again owes the largest amount to CMS ($590 million in 2007 and $2 billion in 2006).

[48] Sources of possible creditable coverage include some employer-based prescription drug coverage, including the Federal Employees Health Benefits Program; qualified State Pharmaceutical Assistance programs (SPAPs); military-related coverage (e.g., VA, TRICARE); and certain Medicare supplemental (Medigap) policies.

[49] The late enrollment penalty is calculated based on the national base beneficiary premium, not the plan's premium. Therefore, the penalty is billed to applicable members even if the plan's Part D basic premium is $0.

[50] http://www.cms.hhs.gov/center/openenrollment.asp.

[51] http://www.medicare.gov/my-medicare-tools.asp.

[52] For example, a plan with the lowest premium and/or no deductible may end up not being the lowest cost plan for the beneficiary if the costs for the beneficiary's drugs are more than under a different plan.

[53] The plans are rated on how well they perform in four different categories, including (1) drug plan customer service, (e.g., how long members wait on hold and how frequently they meet deadlines for timely appeals); (2) member complaints and number of beneficiaries staying with the same drug plan; (3) member satisfaction with drug plans; and (4) drug pricing and patient safety, including how often drug plans update their prices and formulary information on the Medicare website and how similar a drug plan's estimated prices on the Medicare website are to prices members pay at the pharmacy. The ratings range from one to five stars, with one star meaning "poor" and five starts meaning "excellent."

[54] SHIPs are state-based programs that use community-based networks to provide Medicare beneficiaries with local personalized assistance on a wide variety of Medicare and health insurance topics and receive federal funding for their activities. See http://www.medicare.gov/Contacts/static/allstatecontacts.asp.

[55] Medicare Payment Advisory Commission, "Report to Congress, Medicare Payment Policy," March 2009.

[56] http://www.cms.hhs.gov/PrescriptionDrugCovContra/Downloads/CallLetter.pdf.

[57] 73 *Federal Register* 54208.

[58] 73 *Federal Register* 54226.

[59] Medicare drug plan participation in Medicare's enrollment center is voluntary, so not all Medicare drug plans will offer this option.

[60] In a December 2008 report, GAO found that about 15% of beneficiaries who chose to switch plans in the 2008 AEP were not fully enrolled in their new plan by January 1, due largely to the volume of applications submitted late in the AEP. As a result, beneficiaries, pharmacies, and sponsors faced various operational challenges, including the risk of inaccurate charges and additional administrative burden; "Medicare Part D: Opportunities Exist for Improving Information Sent to Enrollees and Scheduling the Annual Election Period", GAO-09-4, December 12, 2008.

[61] Full-benefit duals who live in another country, live in one of the five U.S. territories, are inmates in a correctional facility, have already enrolled in a Part D plan, or have opted out of auto-enrollment into a Part D plan are excepted from this process.

[62] Laura Summer et al., "Medicare Part D 2009 Data Spotlight: Low-Income Subsidy Plan Availability," Kaiser Family Foundation, November 2008.

[63] CMS can waive the standards in the case of (1) MA-PD plans that operate their own pharmacies, provided they can demonstrate convenient access, and (2) private-fee-for-service plans offering Part D coverage for drugs purchased from all pharmacies, provided they do not charge additional cost sharing for drugs obtained from non-network pharmacies.

[64] Interim final rule published September 18, 2008; 73 *Federal Register* 54226.

[65] The term "applicable number of calendar days" is defined as 14 days for claims submitted electronically and 30 days for claims submitted otherwise. "Clean claims" are defined as those claims that have no defect or impropriety, such as the lack of any required

substantiating documentation, or any circumstances requiring special treatment that prevents timely payment from being made.

[66] The subsidy in 2009 is limited to $1,597.40 per beneficiary.

[67] 2009 Annual Report of the Boards of Trustees, p. 163.

[68] CMS, http://www.cms.hhs.gov/EmployerRetireeDrugSubsid/ Downloads/RDS_Sponsors_ PY08 _10_ 06_08.pdf. The federal government elected not to take the employer subsidy for individuals enrolled in the Federal Employees Health Benefits program or TRICARE on the grounds that it would be merely subsidizing itself.

[69] This approach may have some financial consequences for the employer or union since third-party payments do not count toward TrOOP. Thus, if an employer chooses to pay some of the Part D cost sharing on behalf of its retirees, this would have the effect of delaying the point at which the Part D catastrophic coverage would begin.

[70] However, the only statutorily required activity is that CMS conduct financial audits of one-third of the plans each year. Social Security Act § 1860D-12(b)(3)(C).

[71] CMS, "Medicare Prescription Drug Plan Sponsor Part D Audit Guide," Version 1.0, April 10, 2006.
http://www.cms.hhs.gov/PrescriptionDrugCovContra/Downloads/PDPAuditGuide.pdf.

[72] Medicare Part D Prescription Drug Coverage: Federal Oversight of Reported Price Concessions Data, GAO-08-1074R, September 30, 2008.

[73] CMS, "Prescription Drug Benefit Manual,", chapter 9, Rev. 2, April 25, 2006, http://www.cms.hhs.gov/PrescriptionDrugCovContra/Downloads/PDBManual_Chapter9_F WA.pdf .

[74] 72 *Federal Register* 68700, "Revisions to the Medicare Advantage and Part D Prescription Drug Contract Determinations, Appeals and Intermediate Sanctions Processes," published December 5, 2007.

[75] Ibid.

[76] Kaiser Family Foundation, Medicare Part D 2009 Plan Spotlight: Premiums (November 2008); http://www.kff.org/ medicare/upload/7835.pdf.

[77] Response to Member question, before House Committee on Ways and Means, Subcommittee on Health, March 17, 2009.

[78] CMS, October 30, 2008, Medicare Prescription Drug Benefit Symposium, "Beneficiary Experience," http://www.cms.hhs.gov/PrescriptionDrugCovGenIn/08_PartDData.asp.

[79] Jack Hoadley et al., "Medicare Part D 2009 Data Spotlight: The Coverage Gap," Kaiser Family Foundation, November 2008.

[80] Ibid.

[81] James D. Reschovsky and Laurie E. Felland, Center For Studying Health System Change, "Access to Prescription Drugs for Medicare Beneficiaries," Results from the Community Tracking Study, No. 23, March 2009.

[82] Congressional Budget Office, *Budget Options, Volume 1: Health Care*, December 2008, p. 164.

[83] Lisa Murphy et al., Avalere Health, Christy Schmidt, and Sarah Barber, American Cancer Society Cancer Action, "Network Cost Sharing for Cancer Patients in Medicare, 2009," December 2008.

[84] The higher monthly Part B premium amounts for 2009 are based on 2007 income levels and are (1) $134.90—for single beneficiaries with income $85,001-$107,000 or for each member of a couple filing jointly with income $170,001-$214,000; (2) $192.70—for single beneficiaries with income $107,001-$160,000 or for each member of a couple filing jointly with income $214,001-$320,000; (3) $250.50—for single beneficiaries with incomes $160,001-$213,000 and each member of a couple filing jointly with income $320,000-$426,000; and (4) $308.30—for single beneficiaries with incomes greater than $213,000 and each member of a couple filing jointly income above $426,000.

[85] Congressional Budget Office, *Budget Options, Volume 1: Health Care*, December 2008, p. 164.

[86] CBO estimates that about 1% of Part D enrollees would ultimately decline to enroll in the program or delay enrollment as a result of these higher premiums.

[87] Congressional Budget Office, Letter to the Honorable Ron Wyden regarding Medicare's ability to negotiate prices for drugs covered by Part D, April 10, 2007.

[88] Government Accountability Office, "Medicare Part D Prescription Drug Coverage: Federal Oversight of Reported Price Concessions Data" (GAO-08-1074R), September 30, 2008.

[89] Congressional Budget Office, Letter to the Honorable Joe Barton and the Honorable Jim McCrery on the public disclosure of price rebates, March 12, 2007.

[90] Congressional Budget Office, Options for Health Reform, December 2008.

[91] Milliman, Medicare Part D Administrator Survey: Potential Cost Impacts Resulting from CMS Guidance on "Special Protections for Six Protected Drug Classifications" and Section 176 of the Medicare Improvements for Patients and Providers Act of 2008 (MIPPA) (P.L. 110-275), October 16, 2008, http://www.amcp.org/amcp.ark?p=AA8CD7EC.

[92] See CRS Report R40374, *Medicare Advantage*, by Paulette C. Morgan, for issues specific to MA.

[93] http://www.cms.hhs.gov/PrescriptionDrugCovContra/Downloads/2010CallLetter.pdf.

[94] "Medicare Part D: Opportunities Exist for Improving Information Sent to Enrollees and Scheduling the Annual Election Period," GAO-09-4, December 12, 2008.

[95] In the 2010 call report, CMS indicated that they have initiated an evaluation of all of their annual beneficiary materials for the 2010 AEP and that the agency will look at reading levels, effectiveness and length.

[96] Gruber, Jonathan, "Choosing a Medicare Part D Plan: Are Medicare Beneficiaries Choosing Low-Cost Plans?" commissioned by the Kaiser Family Foundation, March 2009.

[97] Medicare Part D Low-Income Subsidy: Assets and Income Are Both Important in Subsidy Denials, and Access to State and Manufacturer Drug Programs Is Uneven, GAO-08-824, September 5, 2008.

[98] "Medicare Part D: Some Plan Sponsors Have Not Completely Implemented Fraud and Abuse Programs, and CMS Oversight Has Been Limited" (July 2008), GAO-08-760.

In: Medicare Part D and Prescription Drugs   ISBN: 978-1-61122-899-1
Editors: J. L. Davies and B. A. Mason   ©2011 Nova Science Publishers, Inc.

Chapter 2

EFFECTS OF USING GENERIC DRUGS ON MEDICARE'S PRESCRIPTION DRUG SPENDING

Congressional Budget Office

SUMMARY

In 2006, Medicare began offering outpatient prescription drug benefits to senior citizens and people with disabilities in a program called Part D. Unlike other Medicare benefits covered under the traditional fee-for-service program—in which providers are paid an administratively determined price for each covered service (or bundle of services) they provide—prices in Part D are not set by the government. Instead, private plans deliver the drug benefit and negotiate their own drug prices while competing with each other for enrollees.

That framework was intended to provide those plans with incentives to make their drug benefits attractive to potential enrollees and to control their costs. One important way in which they do so is by negotiating with manufacturers of brand-name drugs for rebates. Another important mechanism is managing enrollees' use of prescription drugs—and in particular, encouraging the use of generic drugs. Using differences in copayments and other methods, plans can encourage enrollees to switch from brand-name drugs to their less expensive generic equivalents—a practice known as generic substitution. Plans can also encourage enrollees to switch from a brand-name drug to the generic form of a different drug that is in the same therapeutic class, which is one form of a practice known as therapeutic substitution. (Therapeutic substitution can also include switching from a higher priced brand-name drug to a lower priced brand-name drug in the same class.)

The Congressional Budget Office (CBO) used data from the Centers for Medicare and Medicaid Services on prescriptions filled in 2007 under Part D to assess how successful plans have been in encouraging the use of generic drugs and how much additional savings could arise from the wider use of such drugs. Developing policy tools to achieve additional savings from greater use of generic drugs is a further challenge not addressed in this study.

Potential Savings from Generic Substitution

In 2007, total payments to plans and pharmacies from the Part D program and its enrollees were about $60 billion. The total number of prescriptions filled under Part D was about 1 billion, of which 65 percent were filled with generic drugs, 5 percent were filled with multiple-source brand-name drugs (brand-name drugs that are also available in generic versions), and 30 percent were filled with single-source brand-name drugs (brand-name drugs for which no chemically equivalent generic versions are available). Even though a majority of prescriptions were filled with generic drugs, their lower prices meant that those prescriptions accounted for only 25 percent of total prescription drug costs.

Using the Part D data, CBO estimates that dispensing generic drugs rather than their brand-name counterparts reduced total prescription drug costs in 2007 by about $33 billion. Thus, total payments to plans and pharmacies from the Part D program and its enrollees would have been about $93 billion—or 55 percent higher—if no generics had been available. That analysis holds several factors constant and reflects CBO's assessment (discussed below) that generic entry is unlikely to have a substantial effect on either the price of the brand-name drug or the total quantity (including brand-name and generic versions) of the drug sold.

The savings from using generic drugs accrued to Medicare and its enrollees. In 2007, Medicare made 72 percent of the total payments to plans and pharmacies under Part D, and enrollees paid for the remainder through premiums, deductibles, coinsurance, and copayments. A reasonable judgment is that those shares of payments would also apply to the savings from generic utilization—which translates into savings of about $24 billion for the Part D program in 2007 and about $9 billion for its enrollees. The actual share of savings going to each group could have been somewhat higher or lower, however, depending on a number of factors, such as how the savings altered spending across the various coverage phases of the Part D program.

CBO also analyzed the potential for additional savings from increased generic substitution and found that it is comparatively small. If all of the 45 million prescriptions filled with multiple-source brand-name drugs had instead been filled with their generic counterparts, an additional $900 million— representing less than 2 percent of total payments to plans and pharmacies from the Part D program and its enrollees in 2007—would have been saved. Using their shares of payments to plans and pharmacies to allocate those savings, the Part D program would have saved about $650 million, and its enrollees would have saved about $250 million.

Potential Savings from Therapeutic Substitution

Single-source brand-name drugs accounted for 68 percent of total prescription drug costs under Part D in 2007, even though those drugs accounted for only about 30 percent of prescriptions. Plans could have achieved some savings from that group of drugs by encouraging enrollees to switch to the generic form of a different drug in the same therapeutic class— that is, a drug designed to treat the same medical condition.

The potential to reduce costs by promoting such therapeutic substitution depends on the number of single-source prescriptions that it would be medically appropriate to switch. To assess the potential for such savings, CBO examined potential therapeutic substitution for seven therapeutic classes identified by the Medicare program as providing opportunities for such substitution. If all of the single-source brand-name prescriptions in those seven classes had been switched to generic drugs from the same class, prescription drug costs would have been reduced by $4 billion in 2007, or 7 percent of total payments to plans and pharmacies in that year. Again using their overall shares of payments to plans and pharmacies to allocate those savings, Medicare spending would have been reduced by $2.9 billion, and enrollees' spending would have been reduced by $1.1 billion. As with generic substitution, the actual share of the savings going to either group could have been somewhat higher or lower.

The potential savings from therapeutic substitution to generic drugs could have been higher or lower than those estimates, for two reasons. On the one hand, the reduction in costs in the seven therapeutic classes that feasibly could have been achieved would be less than $4 billion because in many cases it would have been medically inappropriate to switch a prescription from a single-source brand-name drug to the generic form of a therapeutically similar drug. Some drugs in a class either may be more effective than others for some of the population or may not be safe for people with other health conditions. Consequently, a pharmacist must obtain the consent of the prescribing physician before substituting a generic drug for a single-source drug that is in the same therapeutic class but is not chemically equivalent.

On the other hand, savings from therapeutic substitution to generic drugs could have been much higher than $4billion to the extent that other classes of drugs also would have presented options for substitution. The seven classes that CBO evaluated represented only about one-fifth of total prescription drug costs and 15 percent of the cost of single-source brand-name drugs under Part D. Even if the share of drugs that feasibly could have been switched in those other classes had been lower than in the classes that Medicare highlighted, those switches would generate additional savings. Compared with the potential for additional savings from generic substitution, the potential for additional savings from therapeutic substitution was greater both because the savings per prescription were greater (given the relative prices of the specific drugs involved) and because slightly more prescriptions had the potential to be switched.

Policymakers would face several challenges in developing tools to achieve any additional savings from the expanded use of generic drugs—particularly in the case of therapeutic substitution. About half of Part D spending is on behalf of enrollees who have lower incomes and thus qualify for additional subsidies. Policies that used financial incentives to steer enrollees toward certain drugs might not be effective for that population because Medicare pays nearly all of their costs. In addition, plans must meet certain requirements intended to ensure that enrollees have access to the drugs that they need and to prevent the plans from discouraging beneficiaries with high drug costs from enrolling; those requirements limit plans' ability to steer drug use. Finally, it could be difficult for policymakers to design policies so that switches from single-source brand-name drugs to generic drugs were made only when medically appropriate.

Implications of Future Developments

The estimates of actual savings from generic substitution in 2007 and potential savings that could have been realized from greater generic and therapeutic substitution during that year illustrate that using generic drugs in the future can reduce spending under Part D. However, the potential for such savings will vary from year to year depending on many factors, including the extent to which generic drugs and new brand-name drugs enter the market.

Over the next several years, entities that pay for prescription drugs will benefit from a wave of brand-name drugs in high-priced therapeutic classes losing patent protection or other periods of exclusivity, which will allow generic drugs to enter those markets for the first time. Also, relatively few new brand-name drug products are expected to reach the market in the near term. If the current rate of generic substitution is maintained, first-time generic entry occurring through 2012 will generate about $14 billion in additional savings from generic substitution, in addition to the $33 billion in savings calculated above (where both figures apply to 2007 spending patterns). However, potential savings from therapeutic substitution for the classes that CBO considered would be reduced from $4 billion to about $2 billion (also based on 2007 spending). That reduction occurs because some of the prescriptions that would have been shifted to a different generic drug (when generating the estimate for therapeutic substitution in 2007) will have their own generic competitor by 2012; those savings are thus included in the $14 billion figure for additional savings from generic substitution.

Two other important considerations stem from the provisions of the recently enacted legislation on health care (the Patient Protection and Affordable Care Act, as modified by the Health and Education Reconciliation Act of 2010). First and foremost, the coverage gap in the Part D benefit—a range of spending in which many enrollees have to pay all of their drug costs—will gradually be closed. As a result, the total amount of drug spending under Part D, the mix of generic and brand-name drugs used, and the federal government's share of drug spending will all change at least to some degree. In addition, the legislation created a regulatory pathway for approving drugs that are "biosimilar" to brand-name biologic products—drugs that are made from living organisms and that tend to be very expensive. How quickly those biosimilar drugs are developed and used, how they are priced, and whether they will be treated under regulation in the same manner as generic drugs for purposes of closing the coverage gap under Part D will all have important implications for future prescription drug spending.

In 2006, Medicare began offering outpatient prescription drug benefits to senior citizens and people with disabilities through the Medicare Prescription Drug Benefit Program (Part D). The program relies upon private plans to deliver those benefits to its enrollees. In contrast to the traditional fee-for-service programs employed to deliver other Medicare benefits—in which providers of health care are paid an administratively determined price for each covered service, or bundle of services, that enrollees receive—prices in Part D are negotiated by private plans that compete with one another for enrollees. That framework was intended to give plans incentives to make their drug benefits attractive to potential enrollees and to control costs. Toward that end, plans use various techniques to manage enrollees' use of drugs and to negotiate price rebates from drug manufacturers and discounts from pharmacies.

Generic substitution, the practice of switching a prescription from a brand-name drug to a less expensive chemically equivalent generic drug, is one prominent approach to controlling costs.[1] This analysis uses data provided by the Centers for Medicare and Medicaid Services (CMS) on prescriptions filled under Part D in 2007 to assess the extent to which generic substitution reduced prescription drug spending in that year. The study also provides estimates of how much more spending could have been reduced in 2007 by additional generic substitution and by one form of another practice—known as therapeutic substitution—in which a prescription is switched from a brand-name drug to the generic form of a different drug that is in the same therapeutic class. In addition, the outlook for future savings from using generic drugs is briefly discussed. To explain who benefits from lower prescription drug spending and the incentives of enrollees and private plans to control such spending, the study begins by describing the design of the Part D benefit, the distribution of spending under Part D, and the role of private plans in the Part D program.

Overview of the Medicare Prescription Drug Benefit Program

Medicare Part D has about 28 million enrollees, and the Congressional Budget Office (CBO) estimates that net outlays will amount to $48 billion in fiscal year 2010.[2] The program as it existed during its first five years is described below, with a particular focus on 2007 because this study uses detailed data from that year. The health care legislation enacted in March 2010 makes changes to Part D that will be phased in over a 10-year period.[3] The changes expected in 2011 and beyond from that legislation are also described.

Design of the Medicare Prescription Drug Benefit

The Medicare prescription drug benefit is delivered by private plans. Private prescription drug plans—sometimes called "stand-alone" drug plans—offer only prescription drug coverage and are designed for enrollees who get their other Medicare benefits in the traditional fee-for-service program. In addition, private health plans, called Medicare Advantage plans, offer prescription drug coverage that is integrated with the health care coverage they provide to Medicare beneficiaries under Part C.[4]

Original Benefit Design. Before the recent enactment of health care legislation, the Part D standard prescription drug benefit included these phases of coverage:

- deductible paid by the beneficiary ($265 in 2007);
- Coverage paid by the plan for 75 percent of drug costs between the deductible and the initial coverage limit ($2,400 in 2007);
- A coverage gap beyond the initial coverage limit in which no further coverage is provided until an enrollee has incurred out-of-pocket drug costs for the year exceeding the catastrophic threshold ($3,850 in 2007, which corresponds to about $5,450 in total drug spending for someone who has no supplemental drug coverage); and
- Coverage of about 95 percent of drug costs beyond that threshold, with 15 percent of those costs paid by the plan and 80 percent paid by the Part D program. That coverage is not capped.

Over time, the dollar values that set those thresholds are indexed to growth in drug spending per enrollee, so that the benefit covers roughly the same share of drug costs from year to year.

Plans may offer the standard benefit established in law, alternative prescription drug benefits that are actuarially equivalent to the standard prescription drug benefit, or benefits that are enhanced in some way. The standard benefit establishes the minimal level of coverage within Part D, but most people receive benefits that have different cost-sharing requirements—such as having a copayment that is a fixed dollar amount per prescription rather than a percentage of the prescription's cost. To be actuarially equivalent, an alternative benefit design must cover the same share of enrollees' drug costs, on average, as the standard benefit. Enhanced plans have a higher actuarial value.

For enrollees in stand-alone plans in 2007, about 20 percent were in standard benefit plans, 60 percent were in actuarially equivalent plans, and 20 percent were in enhanced benefit plans. By 2009, about 10 percent of enrollees in stand-alone plans were in standard benefit plans, 64 percent were in actuarially equivalent plans, and 26 percent were in enhanced benefit plans. Enrollees in Medicare Advantage plans were predominantly in enhanced benefit plans (80 percent in 2007 and 94 percent in 2009). Only about 1 percent of enrollees in Medicare Advantage plans were in standard benefit plans over that time period.[5]

For each enrollee, Medicare provides plans with a subsidy of about 75 percent of the average cost of the standard prescription drug benefit. (A portion of that subsidy is provided by paying 80 percent of drug costs above the catastrophic threshold, and the rest is made as a per-enrollee payment.) Most enrollees pay for the rest of the benefit and any enhanced benefits through premiums. Enrollees who have low income and few assets, however, may qualify for additional subsidies. For those enrollees, Medicare pays for nearly all of the premiums, deductibles, coinsurance, and copayments and for drug spending in the coverage gap.[6]

Medicare also subsidizes prescription drug plans provided by employers and unions for their retirees. To qualify for that subsidy (called the retiree drug subsidy), the plans must offer benefits that are at least actuarially equivalent to the standard prescription drug benefit under Part D. As long as they meet those requirements, the plan sponsors have complete flexibility over the design of the benefits they provide.

Recently Enacted Changes. The recently enacted health care legislation makes several changes affecting the coverage gap in Part D. Beginning in 2011, manufacturers will be required to provide a 50 percent discount off the negotiated price of brand-name drugs included in a plan's for-mulary—a list of drugs that the plan will pay for—to an enrollee when his or her prescription drug spending is in the coverage gap. Those manufacturers' discounts will be counted toward enrollees' out-of-pocket costs for determining whether they have reached the catastrophic threshold. Enrollees who receive low-income subsidies or are in plans receiving the retiree drug subsidy will not be eligible for the discount (presumably because they would not have faced the coverage gap under prior law).

In addition, and also starting in 2011, plans will provide an increasing amount of coverage under the standard prescription drug benefit for drugs purchased in the range of spending that would have constituted the coverage gap; plans that provide an actuarially equivalent benefit will have to increase their value correspondingly. For brand-name drugs purchased in that spending range, plans will pay 2.5 percent of their cost in 2013, increasing to 25percent by 2020 and beyond. For generic drugs purchased in that spending range, plans will pay 7 percent of the cost in 2011; that coverage will increase each year to reach a total of 75 percent by 2020, where it will remain (see Table 1). As a result, by 2020, enrollees will pay 25percent of drug costs in the former coverage gap, just as they do in the initial phase of coverage.

Table 1. Cost Sharing and Manufacturers' Discounts for Prescription Drugs in the Former Medicare PartD Coverage Gap (Percentage of prescription drug spending)

	Brand-Name Drugs			Generic Drugs		
	Enrollees' Cost Sharing	Plans' Cost Sharing	Manufacturers' Discounts	Enrollees' Cost Sharing	Plans' Cost Sharing	Manufacturers' Discounts
2010	100.0	n.a.	n.a.	100.0	n.a.	n.a.
2011	50.0	n.a.	50.0	93.0	7.0	n.a.
2012	50.0	n.a.	50.0	86.0	14.0	n.a.
2013	47.5	2.5	50.0	79.0	21.0	n.a.
2014	47.5	2.5	50.0	72.0	28.0	n.a.
2015	45.0	5.0	50.0	65.0	35.0	n.a.
2016	45.0	5.0	50.0	58.0	42.0	n.a.
2017	40.0	10.0	50.0	51.0	49.0	n.a.
2018	35.0	15.0	50.0	44.0	56.0	n.a.
2019	30.0	20.0	50.0	37.0	63.0	n.a.
2020 and Beyond	25.0	25.0	50.0	25.0	75.0	n.a.

Source: Congressional Budget Office based on the provisions of the Patient Protection and Affordable Care Act (Public Law 111-148) and the Health Care and Education Reconciliation Act of 2010 (Public Law 111-152).

Notes: Those provisions do not apply to the prescription drug spending of enrollees with low-income subsidies or enrollees who are in plans that receive the retiree drug subsidy. n.a. = not applicable.

Distribution of Spending in Medicare Part D

Enrollees pay premiums to Part D plans and also pay deductibles, coinsurance, and copayments to pharmacies under the program. (Those premiums and cost-sharing requirements may be covered by third parties, such as charities or employers.) Medicare pays a premium subsidy to drug plans for all enrollees and additional subsidies for premiums and cost-sharing for low-income enrollees. All together, those payments to plans and pharmacies totaled $59.8 billion in 2007.[7] (That amount excludes prescription drug spending under plans that receive the retiree drug subsidy.) Enrollees paid 9 percent of that total amount in premiums to plans and 19percent in out-of-pocket payments to pharmacies (see Figure 1), for a total of 28 percent.[8] The Part D program paid 28 percent of the total for low-income subsidies beyond the standard benefit, 25 percent for the standard benefit of enrollees receiving low-income subsidies, and 19 percent for the standard benefit of other enrollees.[9] In sum, the Part D program paid 72 percent of the total. (As a result of the recently enacted health care legislation, the share covered by Part D will increase gradually, reaching 75percent in 2019.)

The contribution from the Part D program differed greatly depending on whether an enrollee received a low-income subsidy. In 2007, 24 million people were enrolled in Part D (excluding those enrolled in plans that received the retiree drug subsidy). Low-income subsidies were provided to 38 percent (or 9 million) of the enrollees.[10] For those enrollees, the Part D program paid nearly all of the payments to plans and pharmacies. For enrollees who did not receive those subsidies, the Part D program paid about 40 percent of the payments to plans and pharmacies.

The Role of Private Plans in Medicare Part D

The Part D program was designed to have private plans compete for enrollees on the basis of price, access to prescription drugs, quality, and performance. Each year, plans submit bids to CMS for the cost of offering the standard benefit to an average enrollee. CMS calculates a base premium using the nationwide average bid and determines its subsidy payments on that basis. (Steps that reduce the average bid thus reduce Medicare's costs.) Enrollees must pay the base premium plus any difference between their plan's bid and the nationwide average bid. Thus, enrollees in costlier plans face higher-than-average premiums for standard Part D benefits, and enrollees in less expensive plans pay lower-than-average premiums.

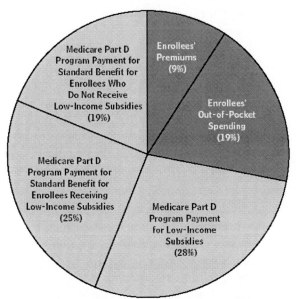

Source: Congressional Budget Office based on Medicare Board of Trustees, *2010 Annual Report of the Boards of Trustees of the Federal Hospital Insurance and Federal Supplementary Medical Insurance Trust Funds* (August 5, 2010), p. 186, Table IV.B10, and p. 189, Table IV.B11; information from the Office of the Actuary at the Centers for Medicare and Medicaid Services; and claims data (Prescription Drug Event data) reported to the Centers for Medicare and Medicaid Services by plans.

Notes: In dollars, the total payments to plans and pharmacies ($59.8 billion) breaks down into the following categories: $5.5 billion for enrollees' premiums, $11.4 billion for enrollees' out-of-pocket spending, $16.8 billion for the Medicare Part D program benefit for low-income subsidies, $14.6 billion for the Medicare Part D program payment for the standard benefit for enrollees receiving those subsidies, and $11.5 billion for the Medicare Part D program payment for the standard benefit for other enrollees.

Enrollees' out-of-pocket spending includes spending by other organizations (such as charitable organizations) on an enrollee's behalf.

Medicare Part D program payments for low-income subsidies include payments for premiums made by the Part D program to plans on behalf of enrollees receiving low-income subsidies.

Medicare Part D program payments exclude payments made under the retiree drug subsidy; those payments totaled about $4 billion in 2007.

Figure 1. Distribution of Payments to Plans and Pharmacies for Enrollees' Prescription Drug Spending Under Medicare Part D, 2007

Plans try to reduce the cost of providing Part D benefits by managing enrollees' use of prescription drugs, by negotiating rebates with manufacturers of brand-name drugs, and by negotiating payment rates with pharmacies. Plans can perform those functions within their organization, but often they contract them out to pharmacy benefit managers (PBMs)—similar to the way that private health plans, including health maintenance organizations and employers' plans, often use PBMs to manage pharmacy benefits on their behalf.

Manage Enrollees' Use of Prescription Drugs. Many plans use tiered copayments to give enrollees incentives to follow a plan's formulary and to use less expensive drugs. A three-tier copayment structure is common: Enrollees pay a low copayment for generic drugs (the first tier), a higher one for preferred brand-name drugs (the second tier), and the highest copayment for nonpreferred brand-name drugs (the third tier). In 2007, the median copayments for stand-alone prescription drug plans were $5 for generic drugs, $28 for preferred brand-name drugs, and $60 for nonpreferred brand-name drugs.[11] (In the coverage gap, many enrollees must pay the full price for their drugs, so they may have even stronger financial incentives to use less costly drugs.)

Plans may also combine formularies with other rules—such as step therapy and prior authorization—to manage enrollees' use of prescription drugs. Step therapy requires that enrollees try a cheaper generic drug or preferred brand-name drug before using a more expensive non-preferred brand-name drug. The use of nonpreferred brand-name drugs may also require prior authorization from the plan, meaning that an enrollee's physician may have to explain why a more costly nonpreferred drug is required over a lower-cost generic or preferred brand.

About half of total prescription drug spending under Part D is on behalf of enrollees with low-income subsidies. Because those enrollees have very little cost sharing, a tiered copayment structure that relies on financial incentives may not be as effective in steering their drug use. Even so, rules such as step therapy and prior authorization could still be used to manage their drug use.

Negotiate Rebates with Manufacturers. Plans (or PBMs acting on their behalf) also use formularies to negotiate rebates with manufacturers of brand-name drugs. In developing its formulary, a plan determines which drugs are therapeutically similar. Then, for brand-name drugs with one or more close substitutes, the plan negotiates with manufacturers for rebates to be paid to the plan in return for placing manufacturers' drugs on the plan's preferred drug list.

In general, rebates are paid to plans for single-source brand-name drugs that are in classes containing similar drugs from which to choose. Rebates are typically not paid to plans (or are small) for multiple-source brand-name drugs and generic drugs. Once a drug is available in a generic version, pharmacists can dispense either the generic or the brand. At that point, prescription drug plans are not in a position to promote either the multiple-source brand-name drug or the generic version, so they do not typically receive rebates on them.

Restrictive formularies that list fewer drugs in each therapeutic class will generate higher rebates than less restrictive formularies that list several drugs in each therapeutic class, because plans with more restrictive formularies will be better able to steer enrollees to a particular manufacturer's drug and away from the drug's competitors. Plans with more restrictive formularies may be less attractive to enrollees, however.

Pharmaceutical manufacturers paid rebates to prescription drug plans under Part D that totaled about $6 billion in 2007. Costs of single-source brand-name drugs in that year totaled about $44 billion in the Part D program. If the $6 billion in rebates were paid primarily for single-source brand-name drugs, then rebates constituted about 14 percent of the cost of those drugs. (Unless otherwise indicated, figures for total prescription drug costs are net of those rebates.)

Negotiate Payment Rates with Pharmacies. Plans (or PBMs acting on their behalf) negotiate payment rates with pharmacies and seek discounts in exchange for including pharmacies in their networks. Drugs purchased at pharmacies outside a plan's network may not be covered or may require a higher copayment or coinsurance rate.

Pharmacies may be willing to accept lower payments per prescription in exchange for the greater volume of sales that can result from being part of a plan's pharmacy network. The plan's ability to achieve large discounts is greater the more restrictive the pharmacy network. However, like restrictive formularies, an overly restrictive pharmacy network may make a plan less attractive to enrollees.

Restrictions on Private Plans in Medicare Part D. Plans must meet certain requirements that limit their ability to reduce the costs of providing Part D benefits. Those requirements are intended to ensure that enrollees have access to the drugs that they need and to prevent plans from discouraging beneficiaries with high drug costs from enrolling. For example, some requirements concern how many drugs in a category or class of drugs must be covered; others involve having an adequate pharmacy network.

Classification systems for drugs are used by plans when developing their formularies. The classification systems group drugs into therapeutic categories and pharmacologic classes of drugs that work in a similar way or are used to treat the same condition.[12] There are many different classification systems. "Model Guidelines" is one such system specifically developed for Medicare Part D.[13] Plans may adopt the Model Guidelines or may use their own classification system. A plan's formulary must include at least two drugs in each therapeutic category and class and must include all, or substantially all, of the drugs in the following six "protected" categories or classes: anti-convulsant, antidepressant, antineoplastic, antipsychotic, antiretroviral, and immunosuppressant.

Generic Drugs in Medicare Part D

CBO examined the use of generic drugs in Medicare Part D for calendar year 2007 using a sample of claims data containing about 10 million prescription records submitted by plans to the Centers for Medicare and Medicaid Services.[14] (For a description of the claims data used in the analysis, see the appendix.) CBO analyzed how much was saved as a result of the use of generic drugs and the potential for savings from increasing the use of those drugs. The analysis examined savings from generic substitution—substituting a chemically equivalent generic drug for a brand-name drug. It also examined one form of therapeutic substitution—namely, substituting a generic drug for a brand-name drug when the generic is not chemically equivalent to the brand but is in the same therapeutic class. Therapeutic substitution can also include substituting a lower priced brand for a higher priced brand that is in the same therapeutic class, but that approach is beyond the scope of this report. (For information about the role of generic drugs in the U.S. pharmaceutical marketplace more generally, see Box 1.)

Generic Substitution

In 2007, about 65 percent of Part D prescriptions were filled with generic drugs, but those prescriptions accounted for about one-quarter of total prescription drug costs (see Table 2 on page 12).[15] By contrast, 30 percent of Part D prescriptions were filled with single-source brand-name drugs, but those prescriptions accounted for 68 percent of total prescription drug costs. Among Part D prescriptions written for multiple-source drugs (drugs that are available in brand-name and generic versions), more than 90 percent were filled with the generic option. That figure reflects the strong financial incentives for plans to encourage the use of generic drugs and for enrollees to use generics when available.

Table 2. Share of PartD Prescriptions and Prescription Drug Costs, by Drug Type, 2007

Drug Type	Percentage of Prescriptions	Percentage of Prescription Drug Costs
Generic	65	25
Multiple-Source Brand	5	7
Single-Source Brand	30	68
Total	100	100

Source: Congressional Budget Office based on Medicare Part D Prescription Drug Event claims data for 2007 provided by the Centers for Medicare and Medicaid Services and rebate data from the Medicare Board of Trustees, *2010 Annual Report of the Boards of Trustees of the Federal Hospital Insurance and Federal Supplementary Medical Insurance Trust Funds* (August 5, 2010), p. 185.

Note: Multiple-source brand refers to a drug that is sold under a brand name but is also available in generic versions from other manufacturers. Single-source brand refers to a drug that is sold under a brand name and is under patent protection—and thus is available from only one manufacturer (or occasionally from other manufacturers under license from the patent holder) and for which no chemically equivalent generic version is available.

BOX 1. GENERIC DRUGS IN THE U.S. PHARMACEUTICAL MARKETPLACE

Generic drugs are chemically equivalent versions of brand-name drugs that can be approved under an abbreviated regulatory process once the brand's patent or other periods of exclusivity in the market expire (or the patent is successfully challenged). Manufacturers of generic drugs are not required to duplicate all of the costly clinical trials conducted by the manufacturer of the brand-name drug; instead, to gain approval from the Food and Drug Administration (FDA), they must demonstrate only that the generic version contains the same active ingredient as the brand-name version (inactive ingredients may vary) and provides very similar concentrations of the drug in the blood.[1] The FDA maintains that if blood concentrations are the same, the therapeutic effect will be the same, so there is no need to carry out studies for clinical effectiveness.[2] Even so, some groups of physicians have expressed concern that generic drugs may not work as well as their brand-name counterparts. For example, the American Academy of Neurology opposes the substitution of generic anticonvulsant drugs for the treatment of epilepsy without the attending physician's approval.[3]

As a result of the abbreviated regulatory process, several manufacturers of generic drugs typically enter the market when the law allows them to do so. As the number of manufacturers grows, price competition among them increases, and the average price of the generic drug relative to that of the brand-name drug declines. On average, the retail price of a generic drug is 75 percent lower than the retail price of a brand-name drug.[4] Accordingly, generic substitution—substituting a generic drug, when one is available, for a brand-name drug—is a major strategy that health insurers use to reduce their spending on prescription drugs.

Private health insurers can promote generic substitution by using a formulary (a list of covered drugs) combined with tiered copayments, charging the lowest copayment for generic drugs and a higher one for multiple-source brand-name drugs (brand-name drugs that have a generic form available). Some health insurers have formularies that exclude multiple-source brand-name drugs from coverage. However, those sorts of formularies are not very common. One 2004 survey found that about 20 percent of employees in the private sector with prescription drug benefits had no coverage for multiple-source brand-name drugs.[5]

Health insurers have help from pharmacists in promoting generic substitution. Generally, when a drug is available in both generic and brand-name forms, states' laws allow pharmacists to fill the prescription with the generic even when the physician has written the prescription for the brand-name drug. Federal regulations implementing the drug benefit under Part D of Medicare also require pharmacists to notify patients if a generic substitute is available. In most states, however, the pharmacist must obtain the consent of the patient or at least must inform the patient when a generic drug is being substituted. The pharmacist cannot dispense the generic drug if the physician indicates in writing on the prescription "no substitution" or that the brand is "medically necessary."[6]

1. In addition, the generic drug must be identical to the brand-name (or innovator) drug in strength, dosage form, and route of administration. It also must be indicated for the same uses; be bioequivalent; meet the same batch requirements for identity, strength, purity, and quality; and be manufactured under the same standards of the FDA's good manufacturing practice regulations required for brand-name products. See the FDA's Web site, www.fda.gov/Drugs/ResourcesForYou/ Consumers/BuyingUsingMedicineSafely/UnderstandingGenericDrugs/ ucm144456.htm.

2. See "Facts and Myths about Generic Drugs," www.fda.gov/ Drugs/ Resources ForYou/Consumers/BuyingUsingMedicineSafely/UnderstandingGeneric Drugs/ucm 167991.htm.

3. See K. Liow and others, "Position statement on the coverage of anticonvulsant drugs for the treatment of epilepsy," Neurology, vol. 68, no. 16 (April 17, 2007), pp. 1249–1250.

4. That information is based on average prescription drug costsT in 2007 from the National Association of Chain Drug Stores (www.nacds.org/wmspage.cfm? parm1= 6536, accessed January 11, 2010).

5. The Kaiser Family Foundation and the Health Research andT Educational Trust survey employers each year to examine trends in employment-based health coverage. The 2004 survey is the most recent one to include a question about mandatory use of generic drugs when available. See Kaiser Family Foundation and Health Research and Educational Trust, Employer Health Benefits: 2004 Annual Survey (Menlo Park, Calif., and Chicago, 2004).

6. Jack Hoadley,J Cost Containment Strategies for Prescription Drugs: Assessing the Evidence in the Literature (report prepared for the Henry J. Kaiser Family Foundation, March 2005), p. 32.

Those estimates for Part D of the percentage of prescriptions filled with generic drugs (65 percent) and the percentage of prescriptions written for multiple-source drugs that were filled with the generic option (more than 90percent) are similar to estimates from other studies of the U.S. market as a whole and of Medicaid. One study found that 69 percent of prescriptions in the United States were filled with generic drugs at the end of 2008.[16] Another study found that 89 percent of prescriptions written for multiple-source drugs were filled with the generic option under the Medicaid program in 2004.[17] Other industry observers have reported that 90 percent or more of prescriptions written for multiple-source drugs were filled with the generic option under plans in the private sector by 2006.[18]

Savings from Generic Substitution in Medicare Part D

CBO estimates that, in 2007, about $33 billion was saved because a generic drug was dispensed instead of its brand-name counterpart. Thus, total payments to plans and pharmacies from the Part D program and its enrollees would have been about $93 billion—or 55 percent higher—if no generics had been available. The estimate is based on the number of prescriptions filled with a generic drug and the observed difference between prices for brand-name drugs and the generic alternatives. The analysis holds several factors constant and reflects CBO's assessment that generic entry is not likely to have a substantial effect on either the price of the brand-name drug or the total quantity (including brand-name and generic versions) of the drug sold (see Box 2 on page 10).

Box 2. How Competition from Generic Drugs Affects Prices and Quantities of Prescription Drugs

Competition from generic drugs has varied and sometimes ambiguous effects on the quantity of a drug sold (including brand-name and generic versions) and the price of the brand-name version.

Effects on Prices

Researchers have found that the average prices of generic drugs are much lower than the prices of brand-name drugs. As more manufacturers of generic drugs enter the market, the average price of the generic drugs relative to that of the brand-name drug declines, and the market share of the generic drugs increases.[1]

The effect of generic competition on the price of the brand-name drug is less clear-cut. Some studies conclude that the price of the brand-name drug increases because of competition from generics. One explanation for that effect is that some consumers are less price-sensitive than others, especially if they perceive the quality of the brand-name drug to be higher than that of its generic competitors. According to that logic, manufacturers of generic drugs compete among themselves for the price-sensitive consumers; the brand-name manufacturer retains the less price-sensitive consumers and chooses to charge them a higher price for the brand-name drug than the price before generic entry.[2]

Other studies conclude that competition from generics exerts a downward pressure on the price of the brand-name drug. In this story, although the price of a brand-name drug typically increases over time after generics enter the market, the competition from generic entry causes the price of the brand-name drug to increase by less than it would have in the absence of generic entry.[3]

Regardless of how generic entry affects the price of the brand-name drug, the overall effect of generic entry is to decrease the average price of the drug (for brand-name and generic versions) because the prices of the generic drugs are so far below the price of the brand-name drug and because generic competitors capture a large share of the market.

Effects on Quantities

Typically, the total quantity of a drug sold might be expected to increase as a result of competition from generic versions because consumers typically buy more of a good when its price decreases. However, the total quantity of a drug sold may remain unchanged or may decline somewhat after generic competitors enter the market, for many reasons.[4] In response to anticipated generic entry, for example, manufacturers of the brand-name drug sometimes are able to modify it (by creating an extended-release version, for instance) and switch consumers to the modified and newly patented version before generic entry begins. Such a switch would reduce demand for the original drug.

A decline in sales could also result if the brand-name manufacturer decreases advertising for the drug. That often occurs when generic competitors enter the market because the brand-name manufacturer is no longer able to capture all the benefits of that advertising.[5] Consumers may switch to a competing brand-name drug that is still advertised, or consumers with the condition may no longer use any drug therapy. A decline in quantity also could be caused by newer brands coming on the market and replacing the older drug therapy (in which case the decline is unrelated to generic entry).

Researchers have found that the overall effect of generic entry is to lower total spending on the drug (for brand-name and generic versions) because the average price is much lower.[6]

Effects on Estimates of Savings

Based on research about the effects of generic entry, the Congressional Budget Office (CBO) concluded that generic entry is not likely to have a substantial effect on either the price of the brand-name drug or the total quantity (including brand-name and generic versions) of the drug sold. CBO's estimates of savingsunder Part D of Medicare from generic substitution—substituting a chemically equivalent generic drug for a brand-name drug—reflect that assessment. If, instead, competition from generic drugs caused brand-name manufacturers to raise their prices, then CBO's estimates of savings might be too high. Conversely, if competition from generics caused brand-name manufacturers to lower their prices, then CBO's estimates of savings might be too low.

The estimates would also change if generic entry led to changes in the quantity of a drug sold in a specific market. If the availability of cheaper generic drugs caused the total quantity of drugs sold to increase, then the estimates of savings might be too high. If the total quantity of drugs sold declined because consumers switched to modified and newly patented versions of the brand-name drug, then spending on those new versions would offset the estimated savings from generic substitution.

In addition, changes in the marketing strategy of pharmaceutical firms producing brand-name drugs and consumers' response to those changes could affect CBO's estimates. If competition from equivalent generic drugs reduced the incentive of the manufacturer of the brand-name drug to advertise and consumers therefore switched to competing brand-name drugs, then the estimates of savings might be too high (if the competing brand drugs have a higher price than the brand with generic equivalents). Or, the estimates of savings might be too low, if the price of the competing brand drugs was lower than the price of the brand with generic equivalents. Finally, if consumers discontinued drug therapy in response to lower levels of advertising, then the estimates of savings might be too low.

More broadly, if entry by generic drugs had been prohibited—that is, if patents for drugs were essentially permanent—the market for drugs could have evolved in different ways that are very hard to predict. The types of drugs available, their prices, and their utilization rates could differ from the observed experience in ways that are not captured by studies of generic entry. Because of the uncertainties involved in predicting what would happen in that counterfactual case, CBO has not factored those possibilities into its estimate of the savings that have been achieved from generic substitution.

1. See F.M. Scherer, "Pricing, Profits, and Technological Progress in the Pharmaceutical Industry," Journal of Economic Perspectives, vol. 7, no. 3 (Summer 1993), pp. 97–115.

2. See, for example, Henry Grabowski and John Vernon, "Brand Loyalty, Entry, and Price Competition in Pharmaceuticals After the 1984 Drug Act," Journal of Law and Economics, vol. 35 (October 1992), pp. 331–350; and Richard Frank and David Salkever, "Generic Entry and the Pricing of Pharmaceuticals," Journal of Economics and Management Strategy, vol. 6, no. 1 (Spring 1997), pp. 75–90.

3. See, for example, Richard Caves, Michael Whinston, and Mark Hurwitz, "Patent Expiration, Entry, and Competition in the U.S. Pharmaceutical Industry," Brookings Papers on Economic Activity: Microeconomics (1991), pp. 1–66; Jayanta Bhattacharya and William Vogt, "A Simple Model of Pharmaceutical Price Dynamics," Journal of Law and Economics, vol. 46 (October 2003); and Sara Fisher Ellison and others, "Characteristics of Demand for Pharmaceutical Products: An Examination of Four Cephalosporins," RAND Journal of Economics, vol. 28, no. 3 (Autumn 1997), pp. 426–446.

4. See Caves, Whinston, and Hurwitz, "Patent Expiration, Entry, and Competition in the U.S. Pharmaceutical Industry."

5. Ibid.; and Bhattacharya and Vogt, "A Simple Model of Pharmaceutical Price Dynamics."

6. See Caves, Whinston, and Hurwitz, "Patent Expiration, S Entry, and Competition in the U.S. Pharmaceutical Industry."

Based on the data that CBO analyzed, about 600 million prescriptions were filled with a generic drug in 2007. For about 500 million of those, a multiple-source brand-name drug was available. (A brand-name drug is not always available because the manufacturer may choose to exit the market after generic entry.) For those 500 million prescriptions, the average price (weighted by the number of generic prescriptions) of the multiple-source brand-name drugs was $89 per prescription, whereas the average price of their generic counterparts was $23 per prescription. The savings per prescription equals $66—the difference between those two average prices. The savings per prescription multiplied by the 500 million prescriptions yields the estimate of about $33 billion in savings (see Table 3 on page 13).[19]

The $33 billion in savings was shared by enrollees and the Part D program through a combination of lower copayments and lower premiums than would have been charged otherwise, but determining the precise share that accrued to each payer is difficult. A reasonable estimate is that the savings were shared in the same proportion as total payments by those groups to plans and pharmacies in 2007 (see Figure 1 on page 4). On that basis, enrollees saved about $9 billion (or 28 percent), and the Part D program saved about $24 billion (or 72 percent).

The actual split of the savings between enrollees and the Part D program depends on several factors: how the savings from switching to generic drugs affects spending across the different phases of coverage, such as the coverage gap and the range of spending above the catastrophic threshold; the mix of prices and copayments for generic drugs and their brand-name counterparts; and whether the use of generic drugs is different for enrollees who receive low-income subsidies than for the rest of the Part D population. As a result, the shares of savings for enrollees and the Part D program could have been higher or lower. For example, the share of savings that accrued to enrollees could have been higher than 28 percent if the savings from switching to generic drugs reduced spending in the coverage gap disproportionately. Alternatively, the share of savings that accrued to enrollees could have been less than 28 percent if the savings from switching to generic drugs disproportionately reduced spending for catastrophic coverage, because that spending is borne mostly by the Part D program.

Another complication in the analysis stems from the fact that plans were also encouraging therapeutic substitution to varying degrees (if only by using tiered copayments). Consequently, some of the $33 billion in savings attributed to generic substitution was instead a result of therapeutic substitution. However, the amount of savings attributable to each form of substitution cannot be calculated from the available data. Because not enough is known about enrollees' medical histories or the brand-name drugs they might have been prescribed initially, it is difficult to determine when therapeutic substitutions might have occurred.

Potential Additional Savings from Generic Substitution in Medicare Part D. Generic substitution has produced substantial savings for Part D prescription drug spending, but the potential for additional savings from increased generic substitution is comparatively small. If all prescriptions for multiple-source brand-name drugs had instead been filled using generic drugs, about $900 million—or less than 2 percent of total payments to plans and pharmacies from the Part D program and its enrollees—would have been saved in 2007, CBO estimates.

Table 3. Estimate of Realized Savings from Generic Substitution, 2007 (Dollars)

Savings per Prescription	
Average Price of Multiple-Source Brand-Name Drugs Weighted by the Number of Generic Prescriptions	89
Minus: Average Price of Generic Prescriptions	23
Equals: Average Savings per Prescription	66
Total Savings	
Average Savings per Prescription	66
Multiplied by: Number of Generic Prescriptions Filled When a Multiple-Source Brand-Name Drug Was Available (Millions)	500
Equals: Total Savings (Millions of dollars)	33,000

Source: Congressional Budget Office based on Medicare PartD Prescription Drug Event claims data for 2007 provided by the Centers for Medicare and Medicaid Services.

Note: Multiple-source brand refers to a drug that is sold under a brand name but is also available in generic versions from other manufacturers.

Table 4. Potential Additional Savings from Generic Substitution, 2007(Dollars)

Savings per Prescription	
Average Price of Multiple-Source Brand-Name Drugs	89
Minus: Average Price of Generic Drugs Weighted by the Number of Multiple-Source Brand Prescriptions	69
Equals: Average Savings per Prescription	20
Total Potential Savings	
Average Savings per Prescription	20
Multiplied by: Number of Multiple-Source Brand Prescriptions Filled When a Generic Drug Was Available (Millions)	45
Equals: Total Potential Additional Savings (Millions of dollars)	900

Source: Congressional Budget Office based on Medicare PartD Prescription Drug Event claims data for 2007 provided by the Centers for Medicare and Medicaid Services.

Note: Multiple-source brand refers to a drug that is sold under a brand name but is also available in generic versions from other manufacturers.

That estimate was derived as follows. About 45 million prescriptions (or 5 percent) were filled with multiple-source brand-name drugs in 2007. Those drugs were most often dispensed when the difference between the price of the brand-name and generic drugs was relatively small. Specifically, the average price of multiple-source brand-name drugs was $89 per prescription, whereas the average price of their generic counterparts (weighted by the number of multiple-source brand-name prescriptions) was $69 per prescription. The savings per prescription equals the difference of about $20 in the average prices. The savings per prescription multiplied by the 45 million prescriptions results in about $900 million in potential additional savings from generic substitution (see Table 4 on page 14). Again, the analysis holds several factors constant and reflects CBO's assessment that generic entry is not likely to have a substantial effect on either the price of the brand-name drug or the total quantity (including brand-name and generic versions) of the drug sold.

The potential additional savings would have been shared by enrollees and the Part D program, but the amounts that would have accrued to each party are not known. Again, using the average shares of payments by enrollees and the Part D program to allocate those savings, about $250 million (or 28 percent) would have accrued to enrollees, and about $650 million (or 72 percent) would have accrued to the Part D program. Because the additional savings would have come from drugs for which the generic alternative was more expensive than average, however, the savings to the Part D program could have been less than 72 percent if the switch to a generic drug reduced enrollees' spending by a proportionately larger amount. For example, on the basis of the difference between the median copayments in 2007 for a preferred brand-name drug ($28) and for a generic drug ($5) and with other factors held constant, the switch from a multiple-source brand-name drug to a generic drug would have saved the enrollee $23, but the plan would have paid an additional $3. If the multiple-source brand-name drug was nonpreferred, an enrollee's savings from switching to a generic version would have been even higher.

Two considerations, however, limit the applicability of those examples. First, they apply only to prescription drug spending between the deductible and the initial coverage limit on behalf of enrollees without low-income subsidies. Nearly all of the potential additional savings on behalf of enrollees with low-income subsidies would have accrued to the Part D program because that program pays nearly all of their costs. Second, if many enrollees had made such switches, then the average share of drug costs paid by enrollees would have been reduced; although enrollees might have initially captured most of the resulting savings, the calculated actuarial value of the plan could have been increased as a result. In that case, CMS probably would have required plans to rebalance their copayment structures to maintain the same actuarial value as provided by the standard benefit design, which would have shifted some savings from enrollees to Medicare. Therefore, using the current shares of spending on Part D to allocate the savings represents a reasonable approximation of the likely outcome, at least on average.

Therapeutic Substitution

Single-source brand-name drugs under Part D in 2007 cost about $38 billion. Some savings could have been achieved from that group of drugs by switching enrollees from a higher priced brand-name drug to a lower priced brand-name or generic drug that is not chemically equivalent but is in the same therapeutic class, a practice known as therapeutic substitution.

Using a tool called the "Medicare Prescription Drug Plan Finder," CBO analyzed one form of therapeutic substitution—switching an enrollee from a single-source brand-name drug to the generic form of a different drug that is in the same therapeutic class. The main purpose of the Medicare Prescription Drug Plan Finder is to help Medicare beneficiaries compare the total prices of plans on the basis of the drugs they take—counting not only the premium they would have to pay but also each plan's cost-sharing requirements for those specific drugs. The tool also indicates when generic versions of drugs are available and provides information to beneficiaries on lower priced drugs that could be substituted for higher priced drugs in 15 classes and subclasses. The majority of those classes and subclasses are for drugs that treat cardiovascular diseases (for example, high cholesterol and high blood pressure). Also included in the list are classes and subclasses of drugs that treat gastrointestinal diseases and allergies.

CBO calculated potential savings from therapeutic substitution for 7 of the 15 therapeutic classes identified by the drug finder as offering opportunities for such substitution (see Table 5 on page 15). Those seven classes were chosen because they contained at least one single-source brand-name drug and one therapeutically similar drug that was also available in a generic form. There were about 180million prescriptions written for drugs in the seven classes and subclasses in 2007, totaling about $10 billion in prescription drug costs. That amount represents about 17 percent of total payments to plans and pharmacies from the Part D program and its enrollees. About 66 percent of the prescriptions in the seven classes were dispensed with generic drugs, accounting for 36 percent of prescription drug costs in those classes. About 30percent of the prescriptions were filled with single-source brand-name drugs, which were 59 percent of prescription drug costs in those classes (see

Table 6 on page 16). For prescriptions written for multiple-source drugs, 95 percent were filled with the generic option.

Focusing on those seven therapeutic classes, CBO determined that switching a prescription in 2007 from a single-source brand-name drug to a generic drug in the same class would have reduced the cost of each prescription by about 70 percent, on average. On the one hand, the potential to increase savings through therapeutic substitution would have been limited by the number of single-source prescriptions that it would have been medically appropriate to switch. On the other hand, savings might also have been feasible in other classes of drugs, but the difference in prices and the extent of the opportunities for therapeutic substitution would have differed in those classes.

Table 5. Selected Classes of Drugs Analyzed for Possible Therapeutic Substitution

Cardiovascular Agents
HMG CoA reductase inhibitors (statins)
Angiotensin-converting enzyme (ACE) inhibitors
Calcium channel blocking agents, dihydropyridines
Calcium channel blocking agents, nondihydropyridines
Nonselective beta-adrenergic blocking agents
Gastrointestinal Agents
Proton pump inhibitors
Respiratory Tract Agents
Mildly/nonsedating histamine1 (H1) blocking agents

Source: Congressional Budget Office based on information provided by the Centers for Medicare and Medicaid Services.

Notes: The Congressional Budget Office selected these seven classes and subclasses because they contained at least one single-source brand drug and a therapeutically similar drug that is also available in a generic form in 2007. Single-source brand refers to a drug that is sold under a brand name and is under patent protection— and thus is available from only one manufacturer (or occasionally from other manufacturers under license from the patent holder) and for which no chemically equivalent generic version is available.

This analysis excludes combination drugs and drugs that have alpha receptor activity or intrinsic sympathomimetic activity.

Table 6. Percentage of Part D Prescriptions and Prescription Drug Costs, by Drug Type, in Seven Selected Classes and Subclasses, 2007

Drug Type	Percentage of Prescriptions	Percentage of Prescription Drug Costs
Generic	66	36
Multiple-Source Brand	4	5
Single-Source Brand	30	59
Total	**100**	**100**

Source: Congressional Budget Office based on Medicare PartD Prescription Drug Event claims data for 2007 provided by the Centers for Medicare and Medicaid Services and rebate data from the Medicare Board of Trustees, *2010 Annual Report of the Boards of Trustees of the Federal Hospital Insurance and Federal Supplementary Medical Insurance Trust Funds* (August 5, 2010), p. 185.

Note: Multiple-source brand refers to a drug that is sold under a brand name but is also available in generic versions from other manufacturers. Single-source brand refers to a drug that is sold under a brand name and is under patent protection—and thus is available from only one manufacturer (or occasionally from other manufacturers under license from the patent holder) and for which no chemically equivalent generic version is available.

Potential Savings from Therapeutic Substitution in Certain Drug Classes.

Prescription drug spending for single-source drugs totaled about $5.8 billion (net of rebates) in 2007 in the seven classes that CBO considered. In the claims data that CBO analyzed, the price of a single-source brand-name drug was $128 per prescription, on average. Because plans received rebates from manufacturers that averaged about 14 percent of single-source prescription drug spending, the average price of a single-source brand-name prescription minus rebates was about $110. The average price of generic drugs in those seven classes (weighted by the number of single-source prescriptions in each class) was $34 per prescription, or about 70percent lower than the average price of the single-source brand-name drugs. Thus, the average savings per prescription from switching equals $76.

There were 53 million single-source brand-name prescriptions in those classes. If all had been switched to generics from the same class, then multiplying by the savings per prescription would yield a potential reduction in prescription drug spending of about $4 billion (see Table 7 on page 17).[20]

That reduction would have been about 7percent of total payments to plans and pharmacies from the Part D program and its enrollees in 2007. The analysis holds several factors constant and reflects CBO's assessment that generic entry is not likely to have a substantial effect either on the price of the brand-name drug or on the total quantity (including brand-name and generic versions) of the drug sold.

The potential reduction of $4 billion in prescription drug spending would have been shared by enrollees and the Part D program. Again applying the shares of payments by those groups to plans and pharmacies in 2007 (see Figure 1 on page 4), enrollees' spending would have been reduced by $1.1 billion (or 28 percent), and the Part D program's spending would have been reduced by $2.9 billion (or 72 percent). The shares of those savings that would have accrued to both parties could have been higher or lower in actuality, however. In particular, shares of savings for any subset of therapeutic classes could have differed from average shares calculated for all classes.

Table 7. Potential Savings from Therapeutic Substitution for Seven Selected Drug Classes, 2007 (Dollars)

Savings per Prescription	
Average Price of Single-Source Brand-Name Drugs, Net of Rebates[a]	110
Minus: Average Price of Generic Drugs Weighted by the Number of Single-Source Brand Prescriptions	34
Equals: Potential Additional Savings per Prescription	76
Total Potential Savings[b]	
Potential Additional Savings per Prescription	76
Multiplied by: Number of Single-Source Brand Prescriptions Filled When a Generic Drug Was Available (Millions)	53
Equals: Total Potential Savings[b] (Millions of dollars)	4,028

Source: Congressional Budget Office based on Medicare Part D Prescription Drug Event claims data for 2007 provided by the Centers for Medicare and Medicaid Services and rebate data from the Medicare Board of Trustees, *2010 Annual Report of the Boards of Trustees of the Federal Hospital Insurance and Federal Supplementary Medical Insurance Trust Funds* (August 5, 2010), p. 185.

Note: Single-source brand refers to a drug that is under patent protection and is sold under a brand name—and thus is available from only one manufacturer (or occasionally from other manufacturers under license from the patent holder). No chemically equivalent generic version is available.

a. Plans received rebates from manufacturers that averaged about 14 percent of single-source prescription drug costs in 2007.

b. Potential savings are higher than the actual amount would be; in many cases, it would be medically inappropriate to switch a patient's prescription from a single-source brand in one of the seven classes to a generic in the same class.

Medical Appropriateness of Therapeutic Substitution

The savings that feasibly could have been achieved from therapeutic substitution in those classes of drugs would have been smaller than $4 billion because it would have been medically inappropriate, in many cases, to make such switches. Within a therapeutic class, drugs may be approved by the Food and Drug Administration (FDA) to treat different symptoms and diseases. For example, within the class of drugs known as "nonselective beta-adrenergic blocking agents" (used for treating high blood pressure) is a subset of drugs that is also approved for treating migraines. The physician of a patient with migraines may not be willing to write a new prescription for a generic drug in that class of blocking agents if the drug has not been approved by the FDA to treat migraines.

Even among drugs approved to treat the same condition, important differences can exist. Some drugs in a class may be more effective than others, at least for some members of the population. Certain subpopulations—for example, people with liver or kidney disease—may need a specific brand-name drug in a class. In addition, some drugs in a class may have harmful side effects for different patients. Depending on the drug, side effects can range from relatively mild (such as dry mouth and drowsiness) to more severe (such as nausea and headaches) to life threatening (such as seizures, difficulty breathing, and liver damage). Moreover, drugs may have different dosing regimens, and physicians may be concerned about a reduction in patient compliance if they switched to drugs that must be taken more frequently. Also, physicians and their patients may be reluctant to switch to a therapeutic alternative once a condition has been stabilized using a brand-name drug. Finally, physicians' clinical experience with their patients may lead them to conclude that certain patients respond better to a particular drug from a given class.

Reflecting those considerations, a pharmacist must obtain the consent of the prescribing physician before substituting a generic drug for a single-source drug that is not chemically equivalent but is in the same therapeutic class. In contrast, a pharmacist can generally substitute a chemically equivalent generic drug for its brand-name counterpart without contacting the physician.

The claims data that CBO used do not contain enough information to determine the percentage of prescriptions for which therapeutic substitution would have been medically appropriate. That analysis would require detailed information about the incidence of diseases and other conditions in the Part D population and a thorough review of disease-treatment guidelines. However, examining potential savings by class provides some additional insight. Almost all of the potential savings from therapeutic substitution were concentrated in two of the seven classes that CBO examined: Proton pump inhibitors accounted for about 50 percent of the potential savings, and statins accounted for 44 percent. That concentration of savings resulted from the high percentages of prescriptions filled with single-source brand-name drugs in the two classes relative to the others—as well as the large number of prescriptions written for those widely used drugs.

Proton pump inhibitors are used to treat chronic symptoms of heartburn or acid regurgitation (known as gastro- esophageal reflux disease) and to treat and prevent ulcers.[21] Research indicates that drugs in that class are similar in safety and effectiveness when compared at equivalent doses.[22] That finding would indicate that a large share of single-source prescriptions could be switched to generic proton pump inhibitors.

Statins are used to lower cholesterol. High cholesterol can increase the risk of a heart attack and death from heart disease or stroke. Statins differ by how much of a reduction in cholesterol they provide. Enrollees who require large reductions to achieve desired blood concentrations would probably require a brand-name statin.[23] Although one health plan reported that more than 75 percent of patients taking a statin could achieve their cholesterol-lowering goals using a generic statin, specific information on the population of Medicare enrollees taking single-source brand-name statins would be needed to determine if the use of generic drugs could be increased among that population.[24]

Application to other Drug Classes. For other reasons, potential savings from therapeutic substitution could have been higher than $4 billion. The seven classes that CBO examined accounted for only 17 percent of total prescription drug costs in 2007 and only about 15percent of the costs of single-source brand-name drugs under Part D. To the extent that other classes also present opportunities for therapeutic substitution, potential savings would increase. Additionally, this analysis considered just one form of therapeutic substitution. If potential savings from substituting lower priced brands for higher priced brands in the same therapeutic class were also considered, then those savings would increase.

The range of rates for the utilization of generic drugs across plans in Part D may provide some insight into the potential for switching prescriptions from single-source brands to generic alternatives across all therapeutic classes. Although the overall share of prescriptions filled with generic drugs was about 65 percent under Part D in 2007, it generally ranged from about 55 percent to about 70 percent among stand-alone drugs plans, and it reached somewhat higher rates in some integrated health plans—indicating that the degree to which plans are promoting the use of generics over brands varies widely, so there may be room for plans with low rates of generic utilization to increase them.[25] (However, the differences in rates of generic utilization could also stem from differences in the population of enrollees in each plan.)

Comparing Potential Savings from Generic and Therapeutic Substitution

CBO's analysis of claims data from 2007 indicates that the potential for additional reductions in prescription drug spending is greater with therapeutic substitution than with the more straightforward generic substitution—although as noted above, the challenges in achieving those savings may also be greater for therapeutic substitution. In that analysis, therapeutic substitution resulted in higher savings primarily because the cost of a generic prescription was about 70 percent lower than that of a single-source brand-name prescription in the same therapeutic class (for the classes examined), whereas the cost of a generic prescription was only about 20 percent lower than the cost of a multiple-source brand-name prescription, on average.

Several factors explain that difference in potential savings. First, single-source brand-name drugs are generally newer and often represent improvements (real or perceived) over multiple-source brand-name drugs that treat the same condition, and their patent protection thus allows their manufacturers to charge prices that are typically higher than those charged for older drugs; that increases the potential savings from therapeutic substitution. Furthermore, when multiple-source brand-name drugs were dispensed, the prices of their generic counterparts were higher than the average price of all generic drugs that had been dispensed, which limits the potential additional savings from generic substitution. Moreover, the number of prescriptions under Part D that could be switched to a generic drug through therapeutic substitution was slightly greater than the number that could be switched through generic substitution—largely reflecting the extensive use of generic substitution that has already occurred. An offsetting consideration is that it would be medically inappropriate to practice therapeutic substitution in many cases, which is one factor that would reduce the actual savings that could be obtained from that approach.

Policymakers would face several challenges in developing tools to achieve any additional savings from the expanded use of generic drugs—particularly in the case of therapeutic substitution. About half of Part D spending is on behalf of enrollees who have lower income and thus qualify for additional subsidies. Policies that used financial incentives to steer enrollees toward certain drugs might not be effective on that population because Medicare pays nearly all of their costs. In addition, plans must meet certain requirements intended to ensure that enrollees have access to the drugs that they need and to prevent the plans from discouraging beneficiaries with high drug costs from enrolling; those requirements limit plans' ability to steer drug use. Finally, it could be difficult for policymakers to design policies so that switches from single-source brand-name drugs to generic drugs were made only when medically appropriate.

Implications of Future Developments

The estimates of actual savings from generic substitution and potential savings from additional generic and therapeutic substitution in 2007 provide some insight into how much savings could be obtained in the future through the increased use of generic drugs. However, some changes in the pharmaceutical marketplace have already occurred—and many others could occur—that might affect actual and potential savings from the increased use of generic drugs. In addition, changes introduced by the recently enacted health care legislation will direct a larger share of any savings that are achieved to the Medicare Part D program because the program will cover an increasing share of prescription drug spending as the coverage gap closes.

Two factors may hold down prescription drug spending in the near term. First, payers will benefit from a wave of brand-name drugs in high-priced therapeutic classes losing patent protection or other periods of exclusivity, allowing first-time generic entry. Second, relatively few new brand-name drug products are expected to reach the market over the next few years.

A countervailing factor is that analysts expect to see a rapid increase in spending under Part D for a particular category of drugs called biologics. Those drugs, which are derived from living organisms, can be particularly expensive. The recently enacted health care legislation created a regulatory pathway for approving less expensive alternatives to those drugs, but in certain circumstances enrollees in Part D may have limited incentives to use them and drug plans may have limited incentives to encourage their use.

First-Time Generic Entry

Over the past several years, more brand-name drugs have become available in generic form, and the dollar value of sales of brand-name drugs that face generic competition has increased accordingly. Brand-name drugs with U.S. retail sales totaling roughly $21 billion in 2007, representing 11 percent of the U.S. retail market in that year, experienced first-time generic entry in 2008 and 2009 (see Figure 2). Drugs accounting for another $43 billion in U.S. retail sales, representing a further 21 percent of the U.S. retail market in 2007, will be subject to first-time generic entry during 2010 through 2012. Within Part D, the cost of those drugs was about $20 billion—equal to 33 percent of total payments to plans and pharmacies from the Part D program and its enrollees in 2007.

The introduction of more generic drugs increases the amount of savings that could be derived under Part D from their use. If the patterns of generic use and price differentials observed in 2007 were to continue, then 93percent of those brand-name prescriptions would be switched to the generic version at a price 74 percent less than that of the brand-name versions. Applying those percentages to the 2007 data on drug spending yields an estimate of about $14 billion in additional savings under Part D. That amount represents a 42 percent increase in the $33 billion in savings estimated from generic substitution in 2007.

Because those calculations use 2007 data, they represent an estimate of the additional savings that could have accrued in 2007 if single-source drugs that will lose patent protection by 2012 had been available in generic form in 2007. Both of those savings estimates—the $14 billion and the $33 billion—would be higher if calculated for future years because of inflation in drug prices and the likely growth in the number of Part D enrollees and prescriptions filled. Because the price of generic drugs relative to the price of brand-name drugs declines as more manufacturers of generic drugs enter the market, the additional savings from new generic entry would also be achieved over time rather than realized immediately.

Those trends in generic drug entry also affect the estimates of how much in additional savings could be achieved either through more generic substitution or from therapeutic substitution. The calculations above assumed that 7 percent of prescriptions would have been filled with multiple-source brand-name drugs, even though generics were newly available at a price 22 percent less than the price of the brand-name drug. If all of those prescriptions were instead filled with generic drugs, about $300 million in additional savings would be generated from generic substitution. That amount (which was also calculated using 2007 claims data and relative drug prices) represents a 33 percent increase in the $900 million in potential savings from additional generic substitution in 2007.

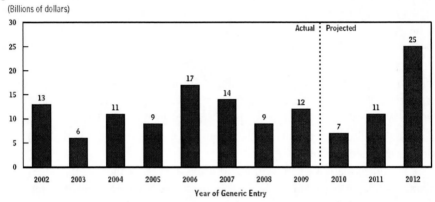

(Billions of dollars)

Source: Congressional Budget Office based on Medco's *Drug Trend Reports* from 2002 through 2010.

Note: For the years from 2002 through 2008, retail sales are reported for the year before generic entry. For the years from 2009 through 2012, retail sales are reported for 2007.

Figure 2. U.S. Retail Sales of Brand-Name Drugs Before First-Time Generic Entry

A further complication is that some of the brand-name drugs experiencing first-time generic entry are in one of the seven classes for which CBO calculated savings from therapeutic substitution. The single-source drugs that will face new generic entry accounted for about $2.5 billion of the $4 billion in potential savings from such substitution estimated for 2007. After that generic entry occurs, savings from those drugs would be included in CBO's estimate of savings and potential additional savings from generic substitution, so potential savings from therapeutic substitution would be reduced by their contribution. In other words, the $2.5 billion in lost savings from therapeutic substitution arises from part of the $14 billion in additional savings that CBO estimated to stem from new generic substitution.

Then again, some of the generic entry that is expected through 2012 will create new opportunities for substitution in three additional therapeutic classes.[26] Although the Medicare Prescription Drug Plan Finder identifies opportunities for possible therapeutic substitutions in those three classes, they were not included in CBO's calculation of potential savings from therapeutic substitution in 2007 because they currently contain only single-source drugs. In other words, the generic drugs in those classes would be first-in-class generics and create opportunities for the type of therapeutic substitution that CBO examined.

However, the potential savings from therapeutic substitution in those three classes would be small. The potential savings associated with entry of those generic drugs was estimated as follows. Single-source brand-name drugs totaling about $0.3 billion in prescription drug spending in 2007 would be candidates for therapeutic substitution. If enrollees' prescriptions for all of those single-source brand-name drugs were switched to the new generic drugs in their classes at a price about 70 percent less than the price of the brand-name drugs, then an additional $0.2 billion would be saved through therapeutic substitution. On net, potential savings from therapeutic substitution in 10 therapeutic classes would decline from the $4 billion calculated for 2007 to $1.7 billion, or by 60 percent. Moreover, in many cases, it would be medically inappropriate to practice therapeutic substitution, which is one factor that would reduce the actual savings that could be obtained.

New Brand-Name Drugs

The rate of introduction of new brand-name drugs is another major factor that will affect potential savings from generic drugs in the future. The introduction of new brand-name drugs can increase the utilization of single-source brand-name drugs and decrease savings from generic drugs, although the precise effect will depend on how big a share of the Part D market the new drugs can capture—and whether they shift drug utilization from existing therapies or largely establish new categories of spending. New drugs that are first in class (or breakthrough drugs) and treat a high-prevalence condition among Part D enrollees could gain a significant share of the Part D market. If enrollees switch from generic drugs to those new drugs, the opportunities for generic substitution would decline—at least until the new single-source drug loses patent protection. Moreover, if the new drug is truly superior, then opportunities for therapeutic substitution would not arise. Conversely, new drugs that enter into a crowded therapeutic class and that have little benefit over existing therapies for most people or that treat a low-prevalence condition among Part D enrollees may not gain much of a share of the Part D market and thus may have only a limited impact on projected savings from using generic drugs.

In the near term, first-time generic entry is expected to have a bigger impact on potential savings than the introduction of new brand-name drugs because the sales of new brand-name drugs are expected to be smaller than the sales of existing brands experiencing first-time generic entry.

Biologics

Spending under Part D on the category of drugs called biologics is expected to increase rapidly in the future. Those drugs can be particularly expensive, with prices reaching tens of thousands of dollars per patient each year. Because most biologics are injected or infused directly into the patient, they are more likely to be covered under Part B of Medicare. Consequently, biologics accounted for only about 6 percent of total prescription drug costs under Part D in 2007.[27] Between 2006 and 2007, however, spending on biologics under Part D grew by about 36 percent, whereas total Part D spending grew by 22 percent, according to the Medicare Payment Advisory Commission.[28] A higher rate of growth for Part D spending on biologics is expected to persist because of the continuing rapid increase in the price of biologics (compared with the prices of traditional drugs), greater use of existing biologics, and the large number of biologics under development.[29]

Provisions of the recently enacted health care legislation will partially mitigate that spending increase by creating a regulatory pathway for licensing products that are "biosimilar" to brand-name biologics. Unlike generic drugs, which contain the same active chemical ingredient as the original patented drug contains, biosimilars are similar to—but not exact copies of—much more complex molecules.

Potential savings in Part D from biosimilar drugs may be limited, however, for several reasons. In certain circumstances, enrollees and plans in Part D may have reduced incentives to use biosimilars. The process of designing and manufacturing biosimilars is complex and more costly than it is for traditional generic drugs, so the price discounts for biosimilars will not be as high in percentage terms as those for traditional generic drugs.[30] Specifically, CBO estimated that prices for biosimilars would ultimately be about 40 percent lower than prices of the original drugs—although the higher average prices for biologic products mean that the dollar differences in prices could still be quite large. The ability of plans to steer utilization toward biosimilars will also play an important role in determining the extent to which savings are realized under Part D. One potential constraint to that ability is that enrollees with low-income subsidies make up a disproportionately large share of the market for biologics under Part D. Because that group has nominal cost sharing, plans would probably need to use tools other than cost sharing (such as step therapy and prior authorization) to steer use toward biosimilars.

Another important issue is whether biosimilars will be treated in the same manner as generic drugs under Part D as the coverage gap is filled in. In particular, CMS has not yet issued guidance on how biosimilars will be classified for purposes of coverage determination in the range of spending that (under prior law) represented the coverage gap. If biosimilars are classified in the same category as generic drugs, enrollees without low-income subsidies and their plans may have incentives to purchase brand-name biologics over biosimilars. Because plans would pay a higher share of the cost of biosimilars than of brand-name biologics in that range of spending on behalf of enrollees without low-income subsidies (see Table 1), plans would probably pay more for biosimilars than for brand-name biologics. The discount provided by manufacturers of brand-name biologics will not only reduce costs to plans and enrollees but will also be counted toward the amount of spending required to reach the catastrophic threshold (at which point coverage is borne mostly by the Part D program), whereas no discount would be required of the manufacturer of the biosimilar. Only about 2 percent of enrollees without low-income subsidies reached that threshold in 2007, however, so that incentive will probably have a limited impact on total prescription drug spending under Part D.[31]

APPENDIX: DESCRIPTION OF DATA USED IN THIS ANALYSIS

This Congressional Budget Office (CBO) analysis of prescription drug spending is based on Medicare Part D Prescription Drug Event claims data for calendar year 2007.[32] Plans submit the claims data to the Centers for Medicare and Medicaid Services (CMS), which uses it to calculate a portion of Medicare's payments to plans. Each record in the data indicates a filled prescription and includes information about the enrollee, plan, pharmacy, and drug product dispensed. For this analysis, the main elements of interest are the product dispensed (identified by its national drug code number), days supplied, prices of the ingredients, dispensing fee paid to the pharmacy, and sales tax.

The claims data for 2007 include about 1 billion records, or prescriptions filled. The total cost for those prescriptions was $62.2 billion (including the prices for the ingredients, the dispensing fee, and the sales tax). For this analysis, CBO used a 1 percent sample of the claims data. The sample was constructed by first selecting a random sample of 1 percent of Part D enrollees and then selecting all the records on filled prescriptions for 2007 for those enrollees. CBO matched brand-name drugs with their chemically equivalent generic drugs in the sample using Thomson Micromedex's Red Book database. That database contains a code to identify drugs with common active ingredients, master dosage form, strength, and route of administration. It also contains information on list prices and other descriptive details on prescription and over-the-counter drugs. Using the additional information from the Red Book database, CBO was able to categorize the drugs as generic, multiple-source brand (brands with generic versions available), or single-source brand (brands without generic versions available).

The data do not include information on rebates from drug manufacturers. But according to the 2010 report of the Board of Trustees for the Medicare program, rebates for 2007 were approximately 9.6 percent of total prescription drug costs.[33] Applying that factor to total recorded cost produces an estimate of $56.2 billion for the total prescription drug cost net of rebates in 2007.

Total payments to plans and pharmacies by the Part D program and its enrollees ($59.8 billion) exceeded the total prescription drug cost net of rebates ($56.2 billion) by $3.6 billion in 2007. That difference in part reflects administrative expenses and profits of plans (including the costs of managing the drug benefit, which plans may do themselves or contract out to pharmacy benefit managers). However, that difference also reflects losses that plans incur on supplemental benefits that are offset by payments under other Medicare accounts.[34] The Medicare Board of Trustees estimates that actual administrative expenses and profits were about $4.3 billion in 2007 or roughly 13.5 percent of plans' benefit payments, which totaled about $32.4 billion.[35] Profits and administrative expenses as a percentage of plans' benefit payments are expected to decline slowly through 2019 because increases in prescription drug spending under Part D are estimated to be larger than increases in employee wages and the other input costs that affect plans' administrative expenses.[36]

End Notes

[1] The term "chemically equivalent generic" is used throughout this study to refer to a generic drug that the Food and Drug Administration has determined is identical or bioequivalent to a brand-name drug in dosage form, safety, strength, route of administration, quality, performance characteristics, and intended use.

[2] Figures exclude enrollees in and payments to plans that receive the retiree drug subsidy (a subsidy that Medicare provides to certain prescription drug plans offered by employers and union groups to their retirees). For details, see enrollment data for 2010, available at www.cms.gov/PrescriptionDrugCovGenIn/. Net outlays are spending on payment benefits minus payments from the states and the portion of premiums paid by enrollees through withholdings from Social Security benefits. (When Part D coverage began, the responsibility for paying for drugs for individuals who are enrolled in both Medicaid and Medicare shifted from the Medicaid program to the Medicare Part D program. In recognition of that change, states are required to contribute to Part D a portion of their estimated avoided drug costs for that population.)

[3] Patient Protection and Affordable Care Act (Public Law 111-148) and Health Care and Education Reconciliation Act of 2010 (P.L. 111-152).

[4] In addition to Part D, Medicare consists of Parts A, B, and C, which pay for other health care services for seniors and people with disabilities. Part A covers inpatient hospital stays, skilled nursing facilities, home health care, and hospice care. Part B covers outpatient hospital care, doctors' services, and many other medical services not covered by Part A. The health care services offered under Parts A, B, and D (except hospice care) can be obtained through private health plans operating under Part C. For more information on Medicare, see Hinda Chaikind and others, *Medicare Primer,* CRS Report for Congress R40425 (Congressional Research Service, March 10, 2009).

[5] Medicare Payment Advisory Commission, *Report to the Congress: Medicare Payment Policy* (March 2008), p. 290 and p. 292; and *Report to the Congress: Medicare Payment Policy* (March 2010), p. 287.

[6] Enrollees qualifying for low-income subsidies are liable for additional costs if they choose plans with higher premiums than the limits set by the Centers for Medicare and Medicaid Services. Those limits ensure that enrollees will have at least one standalone drug plan available to them for which they do not have to pay a premium. See Patricia A. Davis, *Medicare Part D Prescription Drug Benefit,* CRS Report for Congress R40611 (Congressional Research Service, June 1, 2009), p. 12.

[7] Total payments to plans and pharmacies of $59.8 billion exceeded prescription drug costs net of rebates in 2007, which CBO estimated at $56.2 billion. The difference between the two amounts, in part, reflects administrative expenses and profits of plans. See the appendix for more details.

[8] Enrollees' premiums are the sum of premiums for the standard benefit and for enhanced benefits that have greater actuarial value. Premiums for the standard benefit (or a benefit of equal actuarial value to the standard benefit) are from Medicare Board of Trustees, *2010 Annual Report of the Boards of Trustees of the Federal Hospital Insurance and Federal Supplementary Medical Insurance Trust Funds* (August 5, 2010), p.189, Table IV.B11, the column labeled "Premiums." For enrollees with enhanced benefits, that report includes only a portion of their premiums—the amount they would have paid if they had received a benefit of equal value to the standard benefit. Information on additional premium amounts for enrollees with enhanced benefits, which amounted to $1.5billion in 2007, was provided by the Office of the Actuary at CMS.

Enrollees' out-of-pocket spending is based on data on prescription drug expenditures and includes spending in the categories "Patient Pay Amount" (amounts paid by enrollees), "Other True Out-of-Pocket (TrOOP)" (for example, amounts paid by a qualified State Pharmacy Assistance Program), and "Patient Liability Reduction Due to Other Payer Amount" (for example, amounts paid by programs for workers' compensation). "True Out-of-Pocket" refers to the requirement that enrollees must generally incur out-of-pocket costs themselves (and not be reimbursed by a third party) for those costs to count toward reaching the catastrophic threshold.

[9] Medicare Part D program payments to plans for the standard benefit are based on information provided by the Office of the Actuary at CMS. Part D program payments to plans for low-

income subsidies are from Medicare Board of Trustees, *2010 Annual Report of the Boards of Trustees of the Federal Hospital Insurance and Federal Supplementary Medical Insurance Trust Funds* (August 5, 2010), p.186, Table IV.B10. They include payments for premiums, deductibles, coinsurance, and copayments made by the Part D program to plans on behalf of enrollees receiving low-income subsidies. Part D program payments exclude those made under the retiree drug subsidy, which, according to the same report, totaled about $4 billion in 2007.

[10] See Medicare Board of Trustees, *2010 Annual Report of the Boards of Trustees of the Federal Hospital Insurance and Federal Supplementary Medical Insurance Trust Funds*, p. 183.

[11] Patricia Neumana and Juliet Cubanski, "Medicare Part D Update—Lessons Learned and Unfinished Business," *New England Journal of Medicine,* vol. 361, no. 4 (July 23, 2009), p. 408.

[12] For example, Lipitor, a top-selling drug that lowers cholesterol, is in the "cardiovascular agents" therapeutic category. That category is further subdivided into pharmacologic classes. Lipitor is in the pharmacologic class "dyslipidemics."

[13] For more about the development of the Model Guidelines, see The USP Model Guidelines Expert Committee and U.S. Pharma-copeia Staff, "Narrative Review: The U.S. Pharmacopeia and Model Guidelines for Medicare Part D Formularies," *Annals of Internal Medicine,* vol. 145 (2006), pp. 448–453.

[14] Claims data from calendar year 2007 were the most recent available for Medicare Part D when CBO's analysis began.

[15] Estimates of generic utilization can vary depending on which database of drug information is used. CBO used Thomson Micromedex's Red Book database to classify prescription drugs as either brand-name or generic. Medi-Span and First DataBank also publish databases of drug information.

[16] Generic Pharmaceutical Association, *Generic Pharmaceuticals, 1999–2008: $734 Billion in Health Care Savings* (May 2009), p. 4.

[17] Department of Health and Human Services, Office of Inspector General, *Generic Drug Utilization in State Medicaid Programs,* OEI-05-05-00360 (July 2006), p. 7.

[18] Statement of Mark Merrit, Pharmaceutical Care Management Association, before the United States Senate Special Committee on Aging, *The Generic Drug Maze: Speeding Access to Affordable, Life Saving Drugs* (July 20, 2006).

[19] The estimate of savings from generic substitution does not include savings from the approximately 100 million prescriptions filled with a generic drug for which there is no alternative brand available because the brand's manufacturer exited the market. Those prescriptions represent about 4 percent of total prescription drug spending.

[20] The potential additional savings from therapeutic substitution are based on the difference between the price per prescription for the single-source brand-name drug and the average price per prescription for all generic drugs in the same therapeutic class. CBO also estimated savings for each class and subclass using other measures: the average price for a 30-day supply of generic drugs, the lowest price for a generic prescription, the lowest price for a 30-day supply of generic drugs, the price of the most frequently used generic prescription, and the price of the most frequently used generic drug based on the number of days supplied. The estimates of savings varied little between methodologies.

[21] Proton pump inhibitors are also available in low doses over the counter. Those versions are approved by the FDA only to treat infrequent symptoms of heartburn.

[22] Kenneth DeVault and Donald Castell, "Updated Guidelines for the Diagnosis and Treatment of Gastresophageal Reflux Disease," *American Journal of Gastroenterology,* vol. 100 (2005), pp. 190–200.

[23] Drug Effectiveness Review Project, Drug Class Review, *HMG-CoA Reductase Inhibitors (Statins) and Fixed-Dose Combination Products Containing a Statin, Final Report Update 5,* Oregon Health and Science University (November 2009).

[24] Emily Cox, Andy Behm, and Doug Mager, *2005 Generic Drug Trend Usage Report* (St. Louis, Mo.: Express Scripts).

[25] Rates of utilization of generic drugs by plan are based on data from CMS (see www.cms.hhs.gov/PrescriptionDrugCovGenIn/ 06_PerformanceData.asp#TopOfPage).

[26] Those additional classes are angiotensin II receptor antagonists and angiotensin II receptor antagonists/diuretic combinations (drugs in those classes treat cardiovascular diseases) and mildly/ nonsedating histamine1 (H1) blocking agents/decongestants (drugs in that class treat allergies).

[27] Medicare Payment Advisory Commission, *Report to the Congress: Improving Incentives in the Medicare Program* (June 2009), pp. 120–124.

[28] Ibid., p. 120.

[29] Congressional Research Service, *Follow-On Biologics: Intellectual Property and Innovation Issues,* CRS Report for Congress RL33901 (January 6, 2010).

[30] Congressional Budget Office, *Budget Options, Volume I: Health Care* (December 2008), pp. 126–128; and cost estimate for S. 1695, Biologics Price Competition and Innovation Act of 2007 (June 25, 2008).

[31] For the percentage of enrollees with spending that reached the coverage gap, see Medicare Payment Advisory Commission, *Report to the Congress: Medicare Payment Policy* (March 2010), p. 289.

[32] The claims data do not include prescription drug spending under plans that receive drug subsidies for retirees. In 2007, those subsidies totaled about $4 billion.

[33] Medicare Board of Trustees, *2010 Annual Report of the Boards of Trustees of the Federal Hospital Insurance and Federal Supplementary Medical Insurance Trust Funds* (August 5, 2010), p. 185.

[34] Some private plans provide Medicare Part D benefits that are integrated with other health care benefits (such as inpatient hospital stays and doctors' visits) traditionally provided under Parts A and B of Medicare. Those plans, called Medicare Advantage plans, are permitted to reduce premiums for prescription drug benefits and offer supplemental benefits using savings on Medicare payments for providing services under Parts A and B.

[35] Plans' benefit payments are for the standard benefit only. They include the Medicare Part D Program Payment for the standard benefit ($26.1 billion), enrollees' premiums for the standard benefit ($4.0 billion), and low-income subsidies for premiums ($2.3 billion). They do not include payments for supplemental benefits and low-income subsidies for cost sharing (deductibles, coinsurance, and copayments).

[36] See Medicare Board of Trustees, *2010 Annual Report,* p. 185, for projections of plans' administrative expenses and profits.

In: Medicare Part D and Prescription Drugs   ISBN: 978-1-61122-899-1
Editors: J. L. Davies and B. A. Mason   ©2011 Nova Science Publishers, Inc.

Chapter 3

MEDICARE PART D AND ITS IMPACT IN THE NURSING HOME SECTOR: AN UPDATE

Haiden A. Huskamp, Tara Sussman Oakman and David G. Stevenson

ABSTRACT

In 2006, the Medicare Payment Advisory Commission (MedPAC) contracted with Harvard Medical School to explore how Medicare Part D's introduction changed the operations of long-term care pharmacies (LTCPs) and nursing homes, as well as implications of those changes for nursing home residents. Based on interviews conducted across a broad range of stakeholders (nursing homes, LTCPs, Part D plans, financial analysts covering the LTCP sector, consultant pharmacists, physicians working in nursing homes, and advocates for nursing home residents), the June 2007 report offered a snapshot of this sector's transition to Part D. In 2009, MedPAC contracted with Harvard Medical School to update this work by conducting a second round of stakeholder interviews, the findings of which are detailed in this report. The report briefly updates changes in the LTCP industry since early 2007 and describes the recent impact of Part D focusing on: Part D plan assignment and selection; PDP formularies and drug coverage; mechanics of dispensing medications to nursing home residents under Part D; and the impact of Part D on drug utilization and health outcomes for nursing home residents.

Since our initial report, stakeholders of all types have gained experience working through issues related to Part D coverage for nursing home residents. In the context of this increased experience and related safeguards adopted by CMS, many of the initial implementation challenges that arose during the transition to Part D have lessened over time. Overall, it seems providers have adapted to the new benefit and learned to work around its limitations. Formulary coverage is generally viewed as adequate for meeting the needs of residents in most cases. Stakeholders have not perceived a change in overall drug utilization nor any adverse impact on resident outcomes, although they agreed that empirical analyses are needed to assess the impact of Part D on health, functioning, and quality of care. Nonetheless, stakeholders continued to describe the Part D program, particularly its reliance on private plans to administer the benefit and its emphasis on consumer choice, as a poor fit for the nursing home setting.

Stakeholders identified challenges in several areas, including:

Residents' choice of plan and annual reassignments when plans lose benchmark status. Annual reassignment of dually eligible beneficiaries when their plans lose benchmark status for the upcoming year can result in significant clinical disruption as well as administrative burden for residents, nursing homes, and long-term care pharmacies. CMS has taken important steps to lessen these disruptions and allow time for changes in medication regimens to be made, but multiple stakeholders of different types described the "churning" of residents across plans from year to year as the biggest challenge associated with Part D at this time.

PDP formulary adequacy and utilization management. Formulary coverage generally was viewed as adequate for meeting the needs of nursing home residents, although stakeholders noted what they consider to be important exceptions. Moreover, several stakeholders noted that utilization management requirements such as prior authorization, step therapy, and quantity limits had increased over the past few years, a trend that is consistent with previous MedPAC-supported research on Part D formularies generally. CMS-instituted safeguards have reportedly helped lessen potential disruption to residents; however, important limitations to these safeguards were expressed (e.g., PDPs may cover a limited prescription fill rather than a 31 day supply if physicians initially fill a shorter duration prescription for clinical reasons). Nursing home stakeholders also pointed to what they perceived to be continuing discrepancies in the information needed to satisfy utilization management requirements across plans and requested greater standardization in these policies.

Financial implications of non-covered medications and withheld co-payments. Due to regulatory requirements for timely medication dispensing for nursing home residents, LTCPs often must dispense medications before payment is assured. Because nursing homes are required to provide all medications in a resident's care plan regardless of coverage, nursing homes and/or the LTCPs with which they contract must absorb the costs of uncovered medications. Nursing home stakeholders reported that these costs are considerably higher than they were prior to Part D and that they have continued to increase over time. Although stakeholders generally noted some improvement since CMS adopted the "Best Available Evidence" (BAE) guidance, nursing home providers, LTCPs, and consultant pharmacists reported continuing concerns about the process for identifying dual-eligible nursing home residents and difficulties in securing payment for copayments withheld before dual eligibility is recognized by the PDP.

Ongoing communication challenges between PDPs, pharmacies, physicians, and NHs. Communication between nursing homes, physicians, pharmacies, and PDPs around nursing home prescribing remains tenuous in the context of Part D. A complicating factor mentioned by LTCP and nursing home stakeholders is that they often are not included by the PDP in key communications about plan assignment and coverage decisions for residents (e.g., around the need for some residents to select a new benchmark plan or the resolution status of prior authorization or other utilization management policies).

On January 1, 2006, Medicare began offering voluntary prescription drug coverage to Medicare beneficiaries, including those who reside in a nursing home, through the Medicare Part D program. Part D, created by the Medicare Modernization, Improvement and Prescription Drug Act of 2003 (MMA), relies on private plans to administer the benefit.

The Part D drug benefit fundamentally altered the nursing home pharmacy market.[1] The most significant changes created by Part D center on the majority of nursing home residents who are dually eligible for Medicare and Medicaid (i.e., "duals"). The MMA shifted drug coverage for duals from Medicaid to Medicare, requiring the enrollment of duals in private Part D prescription drug plans (PDPs). Under Part D, nursing homes and the long-term care pharmacies (LTCPs) with which they contract no longer function primarily under a single state's Medicaid policies but must instead work across multiple plans, each of which generally has different coverage, formulary design, and utilization management.

Part D includes special protections for nursing home residents, but its core administrative reliance on private plans and emphasis on consumer choice is the same across institutional and community settings even though beneficiaries residing in nursing homes differ from their community-based counterparts in important ways. Medicare beneficiaries living in nursing homes are typically frail, suffer disproportionately from multiple chronic conditions, have higher levels of cognitive impairment, and typically take six to ten different medications.[2-4] In addition, medications are dispensed through different mechanisms for nursing home residents relative to community-based beneficiaries, who are primarily served by retail pharmacies: most nursing facilities contract with a LTCP to provide a range of specialized pharmacy services to their residents, including alternative packaging, 24-hour access, specialized compounding, and emergency delivery.[5]

In 2006, the Medicare Payment Advisory Commission (MedPAC) contracted with Harvard Medical School to explore how the introduction of Part D had changed the operation of LTCPs and nursing homes, as well as the implications of those changes for beneficiaries and the Medicare program. A report released in June 2007 summarized findings from a series of stakeholder interviews across a variety of relevant perspectives conducted between November 2006 and January 2007.[1] In 2009, MedPAC contracted with Harvard Medical School to update its 2007 report by conducting a second round of stakeholder interviews. This report summarizes our findings from these interviews.

PROJECT AND METHODS

As for the 2007 report, we interviewed stakeholders across a variety of relevant perspectives and reviewed existing sources of information. Unless otherwise noted, qualitative data collected from these interviews provide the basis for the information we present. A total of 24 semi-structured telephone interviews were conducted between November 2009 and January 2010. Stakeholder groups from which we collected information included nursing homes (n=8 interviews), LTCPs (n=4), Part D plans (PDPs) (n=3), financial analysts covering the long-term care pharmacy sector (n=2), physicians working in nursing homes (n=1), consultant pharmacists (n=2), federal policymakers (n=1), and advocates for nursing home residents (n=3). In many instances, multiple individuals from the same organization participated in a given interview. Separate protocols were developed for each of the stakeholder groups, and interviews were generally 30-60 minutes in length. Selection of stakeholders sought to maximize representation among Medicare beneficiaries (e.g., efforts were made to interview the larger nursing home chains, LTCPs, and PDPs). To examine whether and how perspectives and experience may differ for smaller providers and pharmacies, interviews were also conducted with these types of provider organizations; however, the findings may be less representative of the range of experience across these smaller entities. In response to our request for a stakeholder interview, the American Society of Consultant Pharmacists (ASCP) fielded a survey of LTCP administrators and consultant pharmacists, and we have incorporated information reported in that unpublished survey where applicable.[a] In a written consent form distributed prior to each interview and reviewed verbally at each interview's start, interviewees were assured the information provided would not be identified with them individually or organizationally. The study design, protocols, and consent form were all approved by the Committee on Human Subjects at Harvard Medical School.

The report begins with a brief update on changes that have occurred in the LTCP industry since early 2007, integrating information provided by financial analysts as well as publicly-available information about the sector. The report goes on to describe the recent impact of Part D in the nursing home and LTCP sectors focusing on: Part D plan assignment and selection; PDP formularies and drug coverage; mechanics of dispensing medications to nursing home residents under Part D; and the impact of Part D on drug utilization and health outcomes for nursing home residents.

UPDATE ON THE LONG-TERM CARE PHARMACY INDUSTRY

Our 2007 contractor report provided a general overview of the long-term care pharmacy (LTCP) industry at that time.[1] Below we provide an update to that earlier overview, focusing on changes that have occurred since March 2007.

Market Changes

Over the past three years, there has been further consolidation in the LTCP sector. In July 2007, PharMerica and Kindred (the second and third largest LTCPs at the time) merged, keeping the PharMerica name. Two large pharmacies—Omnicare and PharMerica—now account for approximately three-quarters of the LTCP market. Omnicare serves approximately 1.4 million long-term care residents, including both nursing home and assisted living residents, while PharMerica serves approximately 315,000. Although precise estimates are not available,[b] Omnicare serves around 60% of the nation's 1.7 million nursing home beds, while PharMerica serves around 15%. Market shares for Omnicare and the merged PharMerica have remained relatively constant since Part D was implemented. The remainder of the industry consists of smaller local and regional LTCPs that may individually serve between 50-100,000 beds in an area. Many of these independent LTCPs join together as group purchasing organizations (GPOs) to contract with PDPs. The three largest GPOs are Gerimed, Managed Healthcare Associations (MHA), and Innovatix.

Industry analysts reported that LTCPs have worked to increase efficiencies over the past few years through consolidation and reorganization of administrative and production functions, redeployment of human capital, investments in new technologies, and efforts to better manage their inventories.[c] Analysts noted that prices LTCPs charge to nursing homes for their services, which recently have been a subject of scrutiny by the U.S. Department of Justice,[d] no longer vary much across LTCPs.[6,7] LTCPs now compete primarily over ways of offering better service to nursing home clients, in the form of items like electronic medical record technology, online refill capability, paperless claim entry, and frequency of medication deliveries. Analysts also noted that large LTCPs have recently been trying to strengthen their capacity to address needs of nursing home residents such as large molecule (i.e., biologic) drug delivery systems and intravenous therapies. For example, in 2009, Omnicare acquired Advanced Care Scripts, expanding its capacity to dispense high-cost injectable and oral medications directly to patients.

PART D PLAN ASSIGNMENT AND SELECTION

A central feature of the Medicare Part D benefit is its administrative reliance on private PDPs. Within limits, plans have flexibility to structure their formularies, cost-sharing, and other plan features, with the expectation that plans will compete on price and that informed consumers will select the plan that is best-suited to meet their individual needs. During annual open enrollment periods, Medicare beneficiaries select from the many stand-alone PDPs and Medicare Advantage plans that will offer drug coverage in their region during the upcoming calendar year. Like they do for other Medicare beneficiaries, private plans administer the Part D benefit for individuals who are dually eligible for Medicare and Medicaid ("duals") and for those who are living in nursing homes; however, there are important differences in how these individuals enroll in plans. To ensure continuity of coverage and to mitigate the potential for adverse selection, duals are assigned randomly to PDPs with monthly premiums at or below regional benchmarks, and they can switch to a different plan at or below the benchmark up to once per month.

Although non-dual nursing home residents are not auto-enrolled, they may also switch plans up to once per month.

Random assignment and steering. In both the 2006/2007 interviews and the recent round of interviews, some stakeholders questioned the wisdom of randomly assigning nursing home residents to drug plans, reasoning that some residents inevitably will be enrolled in plans with relatively less generous coverage of the medications they are taking and may not change to a more advantageous plan. More broadly, some of these same stakeholders questioned Part D's emphasis on consumer choice of plans, arguing that the approach is a particularly poor fit for nursing home residents who may have cognitive impairments and may not have family members actively engaged in their medical decision-making and knowledgeable about their care.

Part D guidance restricts nursing home and long-term care pharmacy providers from directing or "steering" residents to particular plans. The policy is designed to mitigate potential conflicts of interest that might arise if nursing homes or pharmacies recommend enrollment in particular plans. Providers may provide objective information to residents, including information about how well particular PDPs cover their medications, but they are not permitted to steer residents to a subset of plans or to distribute information that could be construed as having this aim. Similar to sentiments expressed during our initial round of interviews, some nursing home administrators, resident advocates, and even one PDP stakeholder expressed the view that nursing home staff should be able to assist residents and family members in selecting a plan that best meets their medication needs, including making specific plan recommendations. The rationale for this position centered on the notion that the nursing home is the entity responsible for ensuring residents' care needs are met, that some residents and family members would like (and indeed expect) the nursing home to play this role, and that this could be a superior mechanism to align plan choice with individuals' needs. At the same time, other nursing home providers continued to support the restrictions on steering of residents by LTCPs and nursing homes, stating that such a role could pose a conflict of interest and open providers to the liability related to recommending particular plans. When asked about practices to educate residents' about their plan choices, nursing home and pharmacy providers reported practices ranging from resident-specific assessments of plan-by-plan coverage to the provision of general information about the relative restrictiveness or generosity of particular plans within a market. A similarly-focused 2008 Department of Health and Human Services Office of the Inspector General (HHS/OIG) study found that nursing home administrators and operations directors engage in a range of behaviors to assist their dual eligible residents in making plan choices.[8] Only about 8% of nursing home administrators and staff surveyed indicated that they or their LTCPs steer most duals to a single plan or recommend one plan to each resident. About one-third said that they provided some information about plans to their residents and one-third said that they worked with residents to find a plan through the CMS Medicare Plan Finder.

Nursing home and pharmacy stakeholders posited that residents generally remain in the plans to which they are assigned and that facilities generally have residents enrolled in multiple plans within a facility. One recent conference presentation of preliminary analyses using 2006 and 2007 Medicare data estimated that close to one-quarter of all dual eligibles switched plans during that period, and institutionalized dual eligibles were more likely than community-based dual-eligibles to do so.[9] To date, there have been no analyses of plan switching at the facility- or chain-level, which could help shed light on the extent to which steering may be occurring.

Plan reassignment. Stakeholders of all types (nursing home, LTCPs, PDPs, and others) reported problems associated with plan reassignment of duals from one calendar year to the next. When a benchmark PDP's premium bid for the upcoming year exceeds the new benchmark rate, dual eligibles who had been randomly assigned to that plan will be reassigned automatically to a plan with a premium at or below the benchmark for the upcoming year. For example, approximately 3.3 million duals[e] were enrolled in plans that lost their benchmark status between 2009 and 2010.[10] Of the 409 benchmark plans available in 2006, only 23 percent of these plans were still available to LIS beneficiaries in 2009.[11] Automatic reassignment either occurs to another plan from the same company (e.g., moving from one Aetna plan to another), or – if there is no benchmark option from the same company in the same region – occurs via random assignment. Multiple stakeholders noted that plan reassignments are problematic and can lead to potential disruptions in medication regimens in addition to the administrative burden of this "churn" for nursing homes, LTCPs, and physicians. To mitigate these challenges, the Centers for Medicare and Medicaid Services (CMS) has instituted safeguards for individuals who are newly enrolled in a PDP (including individuals reassigned at the beginning of the calendar year), requiring plans to cover all medications over a 90-day transition period for new enrollees who live in nursing home settings (see below for additional detail).

Benchmark plan exit creates additional complications for duals who were not initially randomized to an exiting plan but instead voluntarily chose that plan (sometimes referred to as "choosers"). When their plan's premium bid exceeds the regional benchmark, choosers may either select a different plan with a premium below the benchmark for the coming year or remain in their current plan and pay the difference between the premium and the benchmark rate. CMS does not automatically reassign choosers. Choosers and their family members or guardians are notified in writing of the issue before the new calendar year starts; yet, many of these individuals reportedly do not choose a new plan and, thus, begin receiving bills for the premium difference in January. Nursing home representatives reported that they and their pharmacies typically learn of this type of situation either when family members begin receiving these bills and contact the facility or when prescription drug claims start to be rejected after individuals are disenrolled from plans for non-payment of the additional premium amounts. In either scenario, nursing homes and pharmacies immediately work with residents and their families to select a new benchmark plan; however, this enrollment does not take effect until the first day of the following month. In the context of this challenge, nursing home providers felt the issue could be handled more effectively if the facility were notified of the potential need for reassignment in the fall at the same time as families.

Stakeholders generally were attuned to a surfeit of plan choices and the related challenges of working across distinct plan formularies, and we did not hear of challenges related to having insufficient choice of plans at this time. However, a few stakeholders raised long-term concerns about benchmark plan availability. In 2010 there are 307 benchmark plans available—102 fewer plans than were available in 2006.[12] In some regions, benchmark plan choice is somewhat limited. For example, in 2009, duals residing in Nevada had only one benchmark plan option, although the number of plans serving the region increased to 5 in 2010.[12] One stakeholder pointed to the narrowing of the risk corridors over time as one reason why fewer plans now serve the dual-eligible market.

PDP-LTCP Contracting. When Part D was first implemented, a key concern was that the program could disrupt the one nursing home–one LTCP arrangement that most facilities had. By all accounts, this concern has not come to pass. However, in our most recent interviews, nursing home stakeholders expressed concern that contractual disputes around pricing (primarily dispensing fees) between the larger LTCPs, which account for a sizable portion of the market, and PDPs could jeopardize these arrangements. In particular, for chain nursing home companies that use a single LTCP provider, contracts would have to be signed with other pharmacies if their primary LTCP vendor could not reach an agreement with a particular PDP.

PDP FORMULARIES AND DRUG COVERAGE

Medicare Part D PDPs maintain formularies for drug coverage, and these formularies vary across plans. Beyond coverage of particular medications, PDPs are permitted to use utilization management techniques, such as prior authorization requirements (i.e., requiring a physician to obtain prior approval for coverage of a particular medication), step therapy requirements (i.e., requiring documentation that a beneficiary has tried one or more lower-cost medications and not had an appropriate response before granting coverage of higher-cost medications that treat the same condition), and quantity limits (i.e., limiting the days supplied of a medication that will be covered within a given period of time), to control drug utilization. In our first round of interviews, stakeholders generally reported that coverage of most medications used commonly by Medicare beneficiaries living in nursing homes was adequate, although some stakeholders noted what they considered to be important exceptions.[1]

Similar assessments were shared during the most recent round of interviews, with stakeholders of different types indicating that coverage generally was adequate to meet most medication needs of nursing home residents. Yet, most nursing home and LTCP representatives also suggested that the use of utilization management requirements for drugs used commonly by this population had increased over the last few years, a trend that is consistent with findings presented to MedPAC in January 2010 about PDP formulary coverage more generally.[13] These stakeholders noted the additional administrative burden these processes can place on nursing homes, LTCPs and physicians and the potential for clinical disruptions these requirements may cause (described in more detail below). When asked about particular medications or classes where coverage was especially challenging, nursing home, LTCP, and consultant pharmacist stakeholders noted difficulties in several areas, including Alzheimer's drugs, atypical antipsychotics, antidepressants, selected antibiotics, erythropoietin medications, sedative/hypnotic drugs, pain medications, angiotensin receptor blockers (ARBs), eye drops, insulins, nebulized inhalants, statins, and intravenous solutions. According to stakeholders who described these challenges, coverage restrictions may be based in clinically appropriate concerns (e.g., around prescribing of psychoactive drugs) and can arise for different reasons. For example, PDPs might cover the antidepressant Celexa and not Lexapro, with some nursing home clinicians with whom we spoke arguing the latter is more appropriate for individuals with Alzheimer's or anxiety. Similarly, PDPs might cover the generic warfarin sodium and not the brand name Coumadin, even though a nursing home medical director with whom we spoke expressed the perception that the former can contain impurities that make it dangerous to prescribe. Importantly, coverage issues can extend to dosage form, as obtaining liquid or rapidly dissolvable forms of some medications for individuals with feeding tubes or swallowing problems was described as challenging. One nursing home clinician described frustration at the potential tradeoff he saw between offering adequate coverage of a liquid medication form and nursing home staff (inappropriately) administering crushed medication into a gastrostomy tube, which may ultimately clog and lead to its necessary replacement. Nursing home clinicians also expressed frustration around quantity limits that may be appropriate in the community setting but that are challenging to work around in nursing homes. For example, some consultant pharmacists reported that quantity limits can be problematic when a nursing home physician attempts to titrate a dose slowly over several days or weeks to stabilize the patient.

It is important to note, however, that utilization management requirements may provide important safeguards in cases where prescribing could be questionable or inappropriate, either due to controversy about efficacy or concerns about risks or side effects. For example, many nursing home stakeholders identified the erythropoiesis stimulating agents as a class of medications for which coverage issues were particularly challenging. In response to studies that found these medications may speed tumor growth and result in earlier death for some cancer patients, the Food and Drug Administration (FDA) issued a safety announcement about these medications in April 2008 that requires them to be prescribed through a risk evaluation and mitigation strategy (REMS) to ensure that all patients and providers are informed about the risks associated with their use.[14]

Stakeholder reports of increased use of utilization management are consistent with reports by the Kaiser Family Foundation and others that have documented greater formulary and utilization management restrictions as a whole in the Part D program since its creation. For example, a 2009 Kaiser Family Foundation report documented that the percent of prescription drugs subject to some utilization management restrictions, such as step therapy, prior authorizations and quantity limits, increased from 18 percent in 2007 to 28 percent in 2009.[15] In a 2008 report by the DHHS Office of the Inspector General, one-fifth of nursing home administrators interviewed reported concern that PDP formularies may not meet all needs of some dual-eligible residents.[16]

CMS formulary safeguards. Several policies have been implemented by CMS to help protect nursing home residents from PDP formulary limits.[f] First, CMS regulations currently require that PDPs cover "all or substantially all" medications in six medication classes, many of which are used commonly among nursing home residents: anticonvulsants, antidepressants, anticancer drugs, antipsychotics, immunosuppresants and HIV/AIDS drugs. Under this rule, PDPs must cover at least one formulation of every molecule in the class.[g] As noted above, though, PDPs are not restricted in the extent to which they may use prior authorization requirements, step therapy requirements, or quantity limits for these medications. Second, as noted above, PDPs are required to cover a 90-day supply of nonformulary drugs and drugs requiring prior authorization or step therapy for new PDP enrollees who reside in a nursing home, including enrollees who are reassigned in the context of their plan losing its benchmark status. Third, CMS requires that PDPs cover a one-time temporary or emergency supply (one prescription fill or up to a 31 day supply) of non-formulary Part D medications for long-term care residents to ensure that residents do not experience a gap in coverage while an exception or appeal request is being adjudicated for a drug requiring prior authorization or step therapy (http://www.cms.hhs.gov/ PrescriptionDrugCov Contra/ downloads/ CY07 transitionguidance.pdf). One nursing home physician emphasized the importance of this particular policy in ensuring timely access to medications, noting that it can address an acute or emerging need quickly and even help avoid unnecessary hospitalizations of residents in some instances. More broadly, a few nursing home stakeholders emphasized the responsiveness of CMS to concerns that arise in the context of the Part D benefit; however, these same stakeholders also noted that assistance often is on an ad-hoc basis and that more systematic solutions to problems might be more effective. One related request of these providers was that CMS Part D guidance be clearly dated and organized on the CMS website.

LTCP formularies. Before the implementation of Part D, LTCPs typically maintained their own formularies and received rebates from pharmaceutical manufacturers based on the volume of prescriptions filled for nursing home residents served by the LTCP. Importantly, these rebate arrangements have been criticized for putting financial considerations ahead of what is best for residents clinically.[h,] [6] Given that PDPs have responsibility for maintaining formularies that govern Part D coverage for enrollees, it was initially unclear whether LTCPs would continue to maintain their own formularies for Part D covered residents. Different types of stakeholders reported that LTCPs continue to maintain formularies, although they reportedly are used primarily to guide prescribing for residents on skilled nursing facility (SNF) stays funded by Medicare Part A rather than prescribing for medications funded under Part D. For these Part A SNF stays, nursing homes receive a prospective payment that covers all post-acute services provided by the facility including all medications dispensed to residents during their stays. For these residents, the nursing home purchases medications directly from the LTCP.

Stakeholders generally expressed the view that LTCPs likely still receive rebates from pharmaceutical manufacturers, although most reported a belief that the magnitude of these rebates had decreased after the implementation of Part D. Starting in January 2007, LTCPs were required to report these rebates to the PDPs with which they contracted, who then passed this information on to CMS. However, CMS suspended the collection of these data beginning in CY2008, stating that these data were not the most effective tools for ensuring "that Part D sponsors receive information necessary to effectively monitor

LTC rebates to ensure that there are no associated inappropriate impacts on formulary drug utilization.[17]

MECHANICS OF DISPENSING MEDICATIONS TO NURSING HOME RESIDENTS UNDER PART D

As described in our previous report, nursing home prescribing depends on a series of communications between several parties, including the prescribing physician, the nursing home, the pharmacy, and – now – the PDP. In our previous interviews, nursing home clinical staff noted several challenges that arose in the context of Part D, including making coverage determinations at the point of prescribing, receiving communication updates on PDP-physician interactions (e.g., around prior authorizations and appeals), and facing limitations in the parties that may contact PDPs on a resident's behalf (e.g., some PDPs allowed nurses and pharmacies to play this role while others limited these interactions to physicians). Although nursing homes and their LTCPs have grown more accustomed to addressing these challenges over the course of Part D, these challenges largely remain in working across PDPs.

Working across PDP coverage limits. Few stakeholders shared experience with the appeals and exceptions process but rather focused more heavily on navigating prior authorization processes and meeting resident needs despite potential gaps in PDP coverage. Nursing home and LTCP stakeholders again reported that prior authorization and other utilization management requirements can be particularly challenging in the long-term care setting because of characteristics of nursing home organization and staffing. When a medication claim is denied by a PDP, the physician plays a central role in completing utilization management paperwork, shepherding the appeals and exceptions process for the resident, or considering an appropriate therapeutic alternative for the resident. Importantly, nursing home physicians often practice primarily off-site and nursing home residents may represent a relatively small proportion of their practice. Many of these clinicians will not have residents' medical records at their primary practice sites, potentially making these processes more difficult. Nursing home, LTCP, and physician stakeholders expressed varying levels of success and frustration in getting medications claims approved by PDPs. One nursing home physician reported that he was "99% successful" in getting past prior authorization requirements and other claims hurdles, a success he felt was due both to his conservative prescribing approach overall and to his concrete explanations of the risks certain coverage limitations could pose to his patients. Others indicated much higher rejection rates, for example, indicating that almost 25% of claims requiring prior approval would be rejected even with what they considered to be proper documentation.

Stakeholders reported that some PDPs allow pharmacists to sign prior authorization forms to expedite this process, but many do not. Similarly, unlike in the retail setting, LTCPs, are usually relied upon by beneficiaries and nursing homes to initiate appeals for drug coverage and inquiries about claim status; yet, PDPs do not have to recognize LTCPs as agents of beneficiaries unless LTCPs have been officially appointed by the beneficiary to act on their behalf. Beneficiaries are able to fill out a form to make this designation but this form is rarely completed, reflecting the challenges of cognitively impaired residents and potentially distant family members. In the ASCP administered survey mentioned above, many LTCP administrators and consultant pharmacists requested that pharmacies routinely be permitted to initiate the prior authorization process on behalf of the physician and patient and that pharmacies be informed about coverage or prior authorization determinations at the same time as physicians (many plans inform only physicians when these decisions are resolved).

In an effort to streamline the administrative processes used across plans and to reduce administrative burden for LTCPs and nursing home staff, CMS developed a model coverage determination request form for requesting a formulary exception or prior authorization approval and requires that all plans accept this form.[18] Nonetheless, LTCP stakeholders with whom we spoke reported that plans often require their own coverage determination form to be completed as well. In the absence of standardized utilization management forms, plans may have disparate information requirements for these requests, further impeding physicians' ability to address these requirements in an effective manner. One nursing home stakeholder also commented that some requirements can be inappropriate or especially burdensome in the context of nursing home residents, for example requiring endoscopy results for coverage of particular proton-pump inhibitors or extensive lab results for coverage of erythropoiesis stimulating agents. As noted above, these requirements may also add valuable safeguards to protect nursing home residents from potential harms of inappropriate prescribing in some cases.

As noted above, stakeholders agreed about the importance of CMS's transition and emergency fill policies in ensuring medication access for residents. However, nursing home and LTCP representatives also identified limitations with these policies with respect to addressing potential formulary inadequacies. For example, nursing home providers in particular expressed frustration that the initial prescription for a drug might be covered as an emergency or transition fill but that the need to obtain prior approval for the *next* dose or even to work with the clinician to identify an alternate therapeutic agent was often not known until the subsequent claim was rejected. A related point is that nursing home and LTCP providers expressed the view that the policy hampered their ability to manage clinical risk in initially prescribing shorter dispensing cycles than 31 days. For example, physicians sometimes initially write a prescription for a duration shorter than 31 days for clinical reasons, such as the desire to titrate the dose of a new medication slowly. However, under the emergency fill policy, PDPs would not be required to cover a full 31 days of medication in this case – only the initial prescription. Accordingly, some nursing home and LTCP stakeholders suggested that the policy should be changed such that PDPs cover a 31 day supply regardless of the number of fills.

A broader point related to working across PDP requirements is that facilities, LTCPs, and clinicians must now work across formularies and policies of several plans within a facility (e.g., in contrast to Medicaid). Several non-PDP stakeholders suggested the approach conflicted with a trait they valued most in the context of nursing home prescribing – consistency. One nursing home representative noted that even though Medicaid coverage could be challenging in particular states prior to Part D, everyone involved recognized these limitations well and worked around them. Although nursing homes, LTCPs, and clinicians are gaining experience with how to navigate effectively across plans (e.g., one physician mentioned prescribing medications that typically have broad coverage across multiple plans), the notion that Part D's multi-plan approach was a poor fit for the nursing home setting came up repeatedly. For example, one nursing home representative expressed the view that all benchmark plans should be required to provide a baseline of coverage that represents an acceptable floor for nursing home residents. A PDP representative recommended reforms that would go even further, for example creating a single national formulary for all nursing home residents or establishing a single plan for nursing home residents in each region and allowing PDPs to bid competitively to offer such a plan. These types of approach would also mitigate the plan transition issues mentioned above.

Financial and administrative challenges of working across PDPs. Compared to the retail pharmacy setting, several administrative and financial challenges arise in the context of Part D in nursing homes. First, medications generally are dispensed to residents prior to payment being assured. Nursing home, LTCP, and clinical stakeholders pointed to regulatory requirements for timely medication delivery to nursing home residents (e.g., within four hours from the time the prescription is received) as generally being too short to complete the necessary administrative processes required by PDPs. In interviews, both LTCPs and nursing homes were particularly attuned to the financial burden of non-covered medications. The reasons for non-coverage can range from drugs not being on a plan formulary to unmet utilization management requirements, such as hitting quantity limits or not getting prior authorization. Nursing home stakeholders reported that these costs are considerably higher than they were prior to Medicare Part D and are continuing to increase. In a DHHS OIG study, 45% of nursing home administrators reported that their facilities paid for at least one Part D drug for dual-eligible residents.[16] Arrangements of financial risk between LTCPs and nursing homes are somewhat sensitive and subject to negotiation, and stakeholders declined to provide specific details. Still, nursing home and LTCP representatives generally indicated that nursing homes typically assume ultimate financial responsibility for non-covered drugs. Thus far, both nursing homes and LTCPs indicated that medication access for residents has not suffered, while also wondering whether this would change in the context of possible SNF reimbursement cuts in the future (e.g., in its March 2010 report,[19] MedPAC concluded that SNF payments were sufficient to accommodate any potential cost growth and recommended that Congress eliminate the update to payment rates for skilled nursing facility services for fiscal year 2011). Nursing homes and LTCPs shared information about various processes used to minimize financial risk and increase mutual trust that both sides are doing due diligence to get the charges reimbursed. One such process is shortened-cycle dispensing, which means filling prescriptions for five or seven days rather than the more typical thirty one day period, although this strategy can face challenges in the context of CMS's emergency fill policy mentioned above. Of note, one of the potential policy changes discussed under health reform is to reduce waste in prescription medications by standardizing shorter cycles for all Part D prescriptions to long-term care residents.[20]

A financial issue that continues to bedevil Part D stakeholders in the context of nursing homes pertains to beneficiary co-payments inappropriately being withheld from medication payments for duals who reside in nursing homes. In particular, despite stakeholder reports that the magnitude has declined relative to 2006 and 2007 levels, some difficulties remain in being able to identify reliably when individuals are (a) full benefit duals and (b) nursing home residents. LTCPs do not charge co-payments to duals living in the nursing home, but they may not be reimbursed for these co-payments if state computer systems do not correctly categorize residents as LIS-eligible. The financial implication of this gap means losing between $2.50 and $6.30 per prescription (depending on whether brand or generic). Some LTCPs and consultant pharmacists reported that the system has improved somewhat because of better identification of LIS patients by states and by CMS and because of improved administrative systems of the larger PDPs. Another reported factor in these improvements is the change in CMS policy to indicate that LTCPs should be reimbursed if they can provide "Best Available Evidence" (BAE) that the resident is eligible for LIS. Still, LTCP and consultant pharmacist stakeholders reported that the collection of BAE information can be "cumbersome" and time consuming and that BAE information often needs to be submitted multiple times before the co-payment is reimbursed. One LTCP representative reported a decrease in the amount of copayments the pharmacy had written off as uncollectable since the BAE rules were implemented, although the pharmacy attributed the decrease primarily to increased labor resources devoted to gathering BAE information over time and to changes in payment practices made by PDPs in response to the threat of litigation by LTCPs.[21] A final area where LTCPs are distinct from retail pharmacy settings pertains to dispensing requirements. Like retail pharmacies, LTCPs receive a dispensing fee for each prescription they fill but representatives report that these fees are inadequate to cover their costs of doing business. LTCP argue that their dispensing costs are higher than in the retail and mail order settings for several reasons related to relevant regulatory requirements, such as unit-dose packaging, 24-hour drug delivery, emergency drug supplies, and handling unused medications. A recent study commissioned by MedPAC and conducted by Acumen, LLC found that dispensing fees for institutional beneficiaries are higher than dispensing fees for community beneficiaries.[22] For example, Acumen, LLC reported that dispensing fees add approximately 12% to median drug prices for institutional beneficiaries over the period 2006-2008 vs. approximately 4-5% for community-residing beneficiaries. A previous HHS/OIG study comparing Part D and Medicaid dispensing fees to local, community pharmacies found that Part D dispensing fees were, on average, two dollars lower than Medicaid dispensing fees.[23] When asked about dispensing fees paid to LTCPs relative to retail pharmacies,

PDP representatives stated that they generally have the upper hand in negotiations with LTCPs, which represent a small portion of their business, although minimum pharmacy access requirements may limit PDP negotiating power to some extent with the larger LTCPs.

IMPACT OF PART D ON DRUG UTILIZATION AND HEALTH OUTCOMES FOR NURSING HOME RESIDENTS

Assessing the clinical impact of Part D in the nursing home sector is one of the more difficult areas to evaluate without empirical data describing drug utilization and other related processes and outcomes for nursing home residents. With this caveat, nursing home and LTCP stakeholders generally posited that – outside of an industry-wide trend toward generics – overall utilization of drugs by nursing home residents had not changed during the course of Part D. As mentioned above, nursing home and LTCP stakeholders further reported that residents generally receive medications in a timely fashion regardless of PDP coverage rules. This finding from our stakeholder interviews was generally consistent with our previous interviews and with a 2008 DHHS Office of the Inspector General Report finding that 93% of nursing home administrators reported that dual-eligible residents were receiving all necessary Part D drugs.[16] Federal regulations require that nursing homes provide all medications included in a resident's care plan, regardless of coverage for services. As a result, prescriptions are filled by the LTCP and then – if the drug remains uncovered – either the nursing home or the LTCP must cover the cost of the medication. One nursing home representative noted that, despite the administrative hurdles, as long as prescribing physicians are cooperative, medication needs for residents can be addressed.

An initial concern about Medicare Part D was that nursing home residents, particularly dual-eligible residents transitioning from Medicaid coverage to a Medicare PDP, might experience adverse health outcomes due to disruption of medication regimens or PDP limits on coverage of medications used commonly in this population. To date, there is only very limited empirical evidence on the impact of Part D on health outcomes or quality of care for this population. A recent study by Briesacher and colleagues using LTCP dispensing records on nursing home residents found that implementation of the Part D program in 2006 was associated with a temporary but statistically significant decrease in average monthly prescription use per resident of about half a prescription.[24] This study did not, however, examine medication switches or discontinuations resulting from Part D, the impact of Part D on resident health or functional outcomes, or the effects of Part D on utilization beyond the first year of the program. A CMS analysis conducted by Acumen, LLC examined 2007 Medicare claims to assess whether beneficiaries who were reassigned to a new PDP for 2007 (after their 2006 PDP exited the low-income subsidy market) experienced adverse health outcomes relative to beneficiaries who remained in their 2006 PDP and were not reassigned for 2007.[25] Using multivariate regression techniques to adjust for differences in demographic characteristics and health histories (i.e., the RxHCC risk adjustment variables), these analyses found no statistically significant difference in mortality, hospital admissions, or emergency room visits between the two groups. Subanalyses of institutionalized beneficiaries reached similar conclusions. This study did not document the extent of medication changes or discontinuations after plan reassignment or the impact of Part D on health and functional outcomes besides mortality, however. The study also did not assess the impact of Part D plan generosity on utilization or health outcomes for nursing home residents. More generally, advocates, physicians, LTCPs, and nursing home representatives did not perceive there to be major adverse health problems associated with Medicare Part D for nursing home residents, potentially because residents typically receive their medications regardless of whether pharmacies or facilities ultimately are reimbursed. Some stakeholders did raise the concern that people are being switched to new medications for non-health reasons (e.g., because of plan and/or formulary changes), possibly increasing the potential for medication errors and other problems related to these switches. Several stakeholders noted that an empirical assessment was necessary to accurately estimate the impact of Part D on long term care resident health and drug utilization.

Medication therapy management (MTM) programs are one tool used by the Part D program with a goal of reducing adverse drug events and improving medication therapy quality. PDPs are required to sponsor MTM programs, which must include an annual comprehensive medication review and no less than quarterly targeted medication reviews, for beneficiaries in three targeted groups: 1) individuals with multiple chronic conditions, 2) individuals taking multiple medications, and 3) individuals expected to incur annual costs for Part D covered drugs that exceed a predetermined threshold (initially, $4000).[26,27] We heard little from stakeholders interviewed about the use of MTM programs for institutionalized beneficiaries. One PBM stakeholder reported that although some PDPs have extended MTM to long-term care residents, MTM had not been a focus for nursing home residents in part because of the overlapping federal requirement for monthly drug regimen review by a consultant pharmacist for nursing home residents. The stakeholder noted that the recent drop in the threshold for the third targeted group above from $4000 to $3000 may result in more nursing home residents receiving MTM services in the future.

Conclusions

Since our initial report, stakeholders of all types have gained experience working through issues related to Part D coverage for nursing home residents. In the context of this increased experience and related safeguards adopted by CMS, many of the initial implementation challenges that arose during the transition to Part D have lessened over time. Overall, it seems providers have adapted to the new benefit and learned to work around its limitations. In general, Part D does not appear to be a front burner issue for nursing home providers (e.g., relative to payment concerns), and resident advocates have not heard about substantial problems for nursing home residents in obtaining needed medications. Nonetheless, most stakeholders continued to describe the Part D program, particularly its reliance on multiple private plans to administer the benefit and its emphasis on consumer choice, as a poor fit for the nursing home setting, while at the same time warning of important challenges that remain. In sum, our stakeholder interviews provided the following central insights:

- The LTCP industry remains competitive, and LTCPs have worked to increase efficiency and lower costs over the past several years. Analysts noted that prices LTCPs charge nursing homes for LTCP services are now similar across pharmacies, with LTCPs competing primarily on services delivered to nursing home clients. Consolidation over the past several years has resulted in a market dominated by two large companies (Omnicare and PharMerica), although smaller and medium-sized pharmacies (often organized through GPOs) play an important role in the market as well. Pharmaceutical manufacturers continue to pay LTCPs rebates based on their volume of prescriptions, although stakeholders reported that these rebates had diminished in magnitude since Part D was implemented.

- A tension between allowing residents and their family members the freedom to choose a drug plan and allowing nursing home providers to encourage enrollment in particular plans persists. Both nursing home providers and resident advocacy organizations requested that nursing home providers be permitted to play a greater role in educating residents and family members about plan differences.
- Formulary coverage is still generally viewed as adequate for meeting the needs of nursing home residents in most cases, although stakeholders again noted what they consider to be important exceptions to overall formulary adequacy for the institutionalized population. Stakeholders also noted that the use of utilization management requirements such as prior authorization, step therapy, and quantity limits had increased over the past few years, a trend consistent with previous MedPAC-supported research on Part D formularies generally. CMS-instituted safeguards have reportedly helped lessen potential disruption to residents; however, important limitations to these safeguards were expressed (e.g., PDPs may cover a limited prescription fill rather than a 31 day supply if physicians initially fill a shorter duration prescription for clinical reasons). Stakeholders also noted that some PDPs allow the pharmacy to sign prior authorization forms, which reduces the administrative hurdles for nursing homes and LTCPs; however, most PDPs do not allow this. Nursing home stakeholders pointed to continued discrepancies in the information needed to satisfy utilization management requirements across plans and requested greater standardization in these policies.
- Annual reassignment of dually eligible beneficiaries whose plan loses its benchmark status for the coming year results in significant disruption and administrative burden for residents, nursing home providers, and LTCPs. The 90-day transition policy instituted by CMS helps to lessen the disruption and allow time for changes in medication regimens to be made. Yet, several stakeholders of different types described the "churning" of residents across plans from year to year as the biggest challenge associated with Part D at this time. Plan exit from the dual eligible market due to loss of benchmark status may be particularly difficult to negotiate for individuals who voluntarily selected one of these plans (as opposed to being auto-assigned to it). Nursing home and advocacy stakeholders reported that these "choosers" are often uncertain about how to respond to notifications about the loss of benchmark status for their plan, and

nursing home providers are not able to assist them in a timely manner because they are not notified about it directly.

- The number of benchmark plans serving dual eligibles decreased by 25% from 2006 to 2010, with some regions having few benchmark plan options in a given year. Although some stakeholders raised concerns about the future availability of benchmark plan options for duals given this trend, others focused more on the confusing number of plan options for residents at this time and the challenges facilities face in working across these plans.

- Stakeholders have not perceived a change in overall drug utilization after Part D's implementation nor any adverse impact on resident outcomes or quality of care attributable to Part D. Yet, stakeholders agreed that empirical analyses are needed to assess the impact of Part D on utilization, health and functional outcomes, and quality.

- Due to regulatory requirements for timely medication dispensing for nursing home residents, LTCPs must often dispense medications before payment is assured by the plan. Because nursing homes are required to provide timely access to all medications in a resident's care plan regardless of whether a PDP covers a drug or has particular utilization management procedures in place (e.g., prior authorization or step therapy), nursing homes and/or the LTCPs with which they contract must absorb the costs of uncovered medications. Nursing home stakeholders reported that these costs are considerably higher than they were prior to Part D, are continuing to increase over time, and remain a source of tension between nursing homes and LTCPs.

- Nursing home providers, LTCPs, and consultant pharmacists also reported continued concerns about the process for identifying dual-eligible nursing home residents and difficulties in securing reimbursement for copayments withheld before dual eligibility is recognized by the PDP. Stakeholders generally noted some improvement since CMS adopted the "Best Available Evidence" (BAE) guidance, while at the same time noting complexities in these criteria and continued difficulty in obtaining timely reimbursement.

- Communication between nursing homes, physicians, pharmacies, and PDPs around nursing home prescribing remains tenuous in the context of Part D. A complicating factor mentioned by LTCP and nursing home stakeholders is that they often are not included in key communications about plan assignment and coverage decisions for residents (e.g., around the need for some residents to select a new benchmark plan or the resolution status of prior authorization or other utilization management policies).

REFERENCES

[1]   Stevenson, DG; Huskamp, HA; Newhouse, JP. *Medicare Part D, Nursing Homes, and Long-Term Care Pharmacies: A Study Conducted by Staff from Harvard Medical School for the Medicare Payment Advisory Committee*; 2007.

[2]   CMS Review of Current Standards of Practice for Long-Term Care Pharmacy Services: Long-Term Care Pharmacy Primer. The Lewin Group, December 30, 2004. (Accessed January 29, 2010, at http://www.cms.hhs.gov/Reports/downloads/LewinGroup.pdf.)

[3]   Avorn, J; Gurwitz, JH. Drug Use in the Nursing Home. *Annals of Internal Medicine 1995*;123(3):195-204.

[4]   Stuart, B; Simoni-Wastila, L; Baysac, F; Shaffer, T; Shea, D. Coverage and Use of Prescription Drugs in Nursing Homes: Implications for the Medicare Modernization Act. *Medical Care* 2006;44(3):243-9.

[5]   CMS Review of Current Standards of Practice for Long-Term Care Pharmacy Services: Long-Term Care Pharmacy Primer. Lewin Group, 2004. (Accessed January 29, 2010, at http://www.cms.hhs.gov/Reports/downloads/LewinGroup.pdf.)

[6]   The United States Department of Justice, Office of Public Affairs. *Nation's Largest Nursing Home Pharmacy and Drug Manufacturer to Pay $112 Million to Settle False Claims Act Cases*; November 3, 2009.

[7]   Nursing Home Providers Agree to $14 Million Settlement in Kickback Case. McKnight's Long-Term Care News, March 2, 2010. (Accessed March 3, 2010, at http://www.mcknights.com/nursing-home-providers-agree-to-14-million-settlement-inkickbacks- case/article/164791/.)

[8]   Memorandum Report to Weems, Kerry: *"Role of Nursing Homes and Long Term Care Pharmacies in Assisting Dual-Eligible Residents with Selecting Part D PLans"*. Levinson, Daniel R, 2008. (Accessed February 2, 2010, at http://oig.hhs.gov/oei/reports/oei-02-06- 00191.pdf.)

[9]   Bishop, CE; Thomas, CP; Gilden, D; Kubisiak, J. *Enrollment of Dually Eligible Beneficiaries in Medicare Part D Plans: Autoassignment and Choice*. In: Gerontology Society of America Annual Meeting. Washington, DC; November 22, 2008. Available at: http://www.

academyhealth.org/files/2009/monday/Bishopc.pdf.

[10] Medicare Part D 2009 Data Spotlight: Low-Income Subsidy Plan Availability. The Henry J. Kaiser Family Foundation, November 2008. (Accessed February 11, 2010, at http://www.kff.org/medicare/upload/ 7836.pdf.)

[11] Resources on the Medicare Prescription Drug Benefit: Medicare Part D Data Spotlights. The Henry J. Kaiser Family Foundation. (Accessed January 30, 2010, at http://www.kff.org/medicare/rxdrugbenefits/part ddataspotlights.cfm.)

[12] Medicare Part D Spotlight: Part D Plan Availability in 2010 and Key Changes Since 2006. The Henry J. Kaiser Family Foundation, November 2009. (Accessed February 11, 2010, at *http://www.kff.org/* medicare/upload/7986.pdf.)

[13] Hoadly, J; Hargrave, E; Merrill, K. *Medicare Part D Benefit Designs and Formularies.* MedPAC January 2010 Meeting, Washington, D.C. (Accessed April 23, 2010 at: http://www.medpac.gov/transcripts/2010 Formulary Analysis for MedPAC - Hoadley.pdf).

[14] FDA Announces New Safety Plan for Agents used to Treat Chemotherapy-Related Anemia. U.S. Food and Drug Administration, February 16, 2010. (Accessed March 3, 2010, at http://www.fda.gov/ NewsEvents/Newsroom/PressAnnouncements/ucm200471.htm.)

[15] Medicare Prescription Drug Plans in 2009 and Key Changes Since 2006: Summary of Findings. The Henry J. Kaiser Family Foundation, 2009. (Accessed January 29, 2010, at http://www.kff.org/medicare/upload/ 7917.pdf.)

[16] Availability of Medicare Part D Drugs to Dual-Eligible Nursing Home Residents. Levinson, Daniel R of the Department of Health and Human Services, Office of Inspector General, June 2008. (Accessed February 11, 2010, at http://oig.hhs.gov/oei/reports/oei-02-06-00190.pdf.)

[17] Memorandum to All Part D Plan Sponsors: "*Changes to Part D Reporting Requirement - LTC Pharmacy Rebate Data*". Tudor, Cynthia G. of Centers for Medicare and Medicaid Services in the Department of Health and Human Services, November 28, 2008.(Accessed February 11, 2010, athttp://www.ascp.com/medicarerx/upload/MemoLTCRebate RptChange.pdf.)

[18] Steinmo, S; Watts, J. It's the institutions, stupid! Why comprehensive national health insurance always fails in America [see comments]. *J Health Polit Policy Law* 1995;20(2):329-72.

[19] Medicare Payment Advisory (MedPAC). *Report to the Congress:*

Medicare Payment Policy; March 1, 2010.

[20] Harris, J. Unprincipled QALYs: a response to Cubbon. *J Med Ethics* 1991;17(4):185-8.

[21] Murray, CJ. Quantifying the burden of disease: the technical basis for disability- adjusted life years. *Bull World Health Organ* 1994;72(3):429-45.

[22] MaCurdy, T; Bounds, M; Ueda, K; Cornwell, A; Jhatakia, S; Son, J. *2008 Price Indices for Part D Prescription Drugs.* Commissioned by MedPAC, conducted by Acumen, LLC. February, 2010.

[23] Memorandum to Weems, Kerry: Review of the Relationship Between Medicare Part D Payments to Local, Community Pharmacies and the Pharmacies' Drug Acquisition Costs. Levinson, Daniel R of the Department of Health and Human Services, Office of Inspector General, January 2008. (Accessed February 2, 2010, at http://oig.hhs.gov/oas/reports/region6/60700107.pdf.)

[24] Briesacher, BA; Soumerai, SB; Field, TS; Fouayzi, H; Gurwitz, JH. Nursing Home Residents and Enrollment in Medicare Part D. *Journal of the American Geriatric Society* 2009;57:1902-7.

[25] Impact of Reassignment in the Part D Program on Health Outcomes. Centers for Medicare and Medicaid Services in the Department of Health and Human Services, June 11, 2009. (Accessed February 11, 2010, at http://www.cms.hhs.gov/PrescriptionDrugCovGenIn/Downloads/ReassignmentOutcomes .pdf.)

[26] Medicare Part D Medication Therapy Management (MTM) Programs: 2009 Fact Sheet. Centers for Medicare and Medicaid Services in the Department of Health and Human Services, July 21, 2009. (Accessed February 11, 2010, at http://www.cms.hhs.gov/Prescriptiondrugcov contra/downloads/mtmfactsheet.pdf.)

[27] What is the Outlook for Medicare Part D 2010? Q1Group, LLC: Education and Decision Support Tools for the Medicare Community, July 2009. (Accessed February 11, 2010, at http://www.q1medicare.com/PartD-The-2010-Medicare-Part-D-Outlook.php.)

End Notes

[a] 230 individuals responded to the ASCP survey. Approximately two-thirds of respondents reported that they were long-term care pharmacy administrators and a little over one-fifth reported that they were employed as consultant pharmacists. No overall response rate was available.

[b] The LTCPs we interviewed did not provide information on the number of residents served by type of care long-term care services the individuals were receiving (e.g., number receiving skilled care vs. assisted living vs. hospice). LTCPs cited proprietary reasons for not divulging detailed data of this type.

[c] For example, one recent effort to increase efficiency undertaken by Omnicare is described in: http//ir.omnicare.com/phoenix.zhtml?c=65516&p=irol-newsArticle&ID=888420&highlight

[d] In November 2009, the Department of Justice (DOJ) announced that Omnicare care would pay $98 million to resolve allegations that Omnicare paid kickbacks to nursing homes by providing consultant pharmacist services at rates below cost in order to induce the nursing homes to contract with Omnicare as well as other allegations that Omnicare had received kickbacks from Johnson & Johnson in exchange for agreeing to recommend that physicians prescribe Risperdal. Omnicare did not admit wrongdoing in these cases. In a separate action, the DOJ made similar allegations about kickbacks for pharmacy services contracts against Omnicare, Mariner Health Care, and SavaSenior Care; Mariner and Sava recently agreed to a $14 million settlement in this case.

[e] Each year, a sizeable number of dual-eligible beneficiaries have been reassigned when their plan lost benchmark status for the coming year. CMS reassigned 1.1 million duals for 2007, 2.1 million for 2008, and 1.6 million for 2009.

[f] Importantly, CMS is considering regulatory changes that would affect the process by which it establishes protected classes in the future and other related protections (e.g., for comments on these proposed change, see http://www.ascp.com/advocacy/upload/120809%20ASCP%20Comments%20on%20Policy%20changes%20and%20 Clarifications.pdf; http://www.thenationalcouncil.org/galleries/policy-file/Comments%20on%20CMS%204085%20P%2012-7-09.pdf).

[g] However, recent legislation codifying the requirement that PDPs must list "all or substantially all" drugs in these six classes allows CMS to establish exceptions that permit PDPs to either exclude a drug in the protected classes from its formulary or impose utilization restrictions (http://edocket.access.gpo.gov/2009/pdf/E9-783.pdf).

[h] As noted above, in November 2009, the DOJ announced that Omnicare would pay $98 million to resolve allegations that it had solicited and received kickbacks from Johnson & Johnson in exchange for agreeing to recommend that physicians prescribe Risperdal to nursing home residents served by the pharmacy as well as other unrelated allegations.

In: Medicare Part D and Prescription Drugs   ISBN: 978-1-61122-899-1
Editors: J. L. Davies and B. A. Mason   ©2011 Nova Science Publishers, Inc.

Chapter 4

DRUGS ON SPECIALTY TIERS IN PART D

Elizabeth Hargrave, Jack Hoadley and Katie Merrell

BACKGROUND

Medicare Part D requires plans to establish a formulary that lists the drugs that the plan agrees to cover and at what level of cost sharing. Although the original standard" benefit package with 25 percent cost to offer a benefit with tiered cost sharing. Plans typically use this flexibility to offer different levels of cost sharing for generic, preferred, and non-preferred drugs. A growing number of plans include an additional "specialty" Most plans use flat copayments for most oftier for very high their tiers (*e.g.,* $5 for generics, $30 for preferred brands), but variable coinsurance for specialty tiers (*e.g.,* 25 percent of the drug's cost).

Specialty drugs are, by definition, very expensive drugs. As it became clear that many plans were using specialty tiers, CMS established a minimum cost threshold drugs must meet before plans can place them on a specialty tier: in 2007, the minimum monthly cost was $500, and in 2008 and 2009, the minimum was $600. Many drugs placed on specialty tiers actually cost much more. Thus, the placement of a drug on a coinsurance-based specialty tier, rather than a tier with a flat copay, can have serious implications for both beneficiary and plan costs. That impact on beneficiaries is constrained, however, because many long-term users of these drugs reach the out-of-pocket limit and qualify for catastrophic coverage. Furthermore, federal reinsurance limits the impact on plan costs by paying 80 percent of costs once plan enrollees qualify for catastrophic coverage.

Part D enrollees have the right to request an exception to- a plan's preferred, but not for drugs on the specialty tier. In general, if an enrollee can establish that a non-preferred drug is medically necessary and no preferred drug would be as effective, the enrollee can pay the lower cost sharing that applies to the preferred drug. Plans are not required to grant tier exceptions requests for drugs on the specialty tier, even if no other drug is available to treat the beneficiary' s condition. Thus, beneficiaries must in all cases pay the full cost-sharing amount for these high-cost drugs. CMS cites this as a policy that helps more predictable. Because data are not available on the use of the tiering exceptions process for drugs on other tiers (such as high-cost non-preferred tiers), it is unclear how many beneficiaries might seek a tiering exception if that option were available for specialty drugs.

SUMMARY FINDINGS

- A substantial majority of all Part D plans use specialty tiers in 2008. The percentage of plans using specialty tiers has increased since 2006: from 63 to 76 percent of PDPs, and from 67 to 90 percent of MA-PDs.
- Most PDPs and MA-PDS with specialty tiers employ either 25 percent or 33 percent coinsurance, with a gradual trend toward higher coinsurance levels.
- About one in five drugs are placed on a specialty tier by at least one plan, but there is not much consensus among plans about which drugs belong on specialty tiers. Drugs that are on a specialty tier for at least one plan are not typically listed on the specialty tier of all plans in fact, fewer than one-fifth of specialty drugs are on a specialty tier in almost all plans. About 40 percent of specialty drugs ever listed on a specialty tier are on such a tier in fewer than half of all plans.
- When not listed on a specialty tier, specialty drugs are most often listed as preferred brand drugs or listed on a plan' s only brand tier.
- Specialty drugs face utilization management restrictions in over one-third of plans twice as much as other drugs regardless of whether they are placed by the plan on a specialty tier. They are over five times as likely as other drugs to be subject to prior authorization.

- Brand-only drugs are much more likely to be placed on specialty tiers, compared to those with generic alternatives, and injectible drugs are much more likely than oral solids to be on specialty tiers.
- Drugs in just four classes (antineoplastics, immunologics, antivirals, and antibacterials) account for nearly two-thirds of specialty drugs.

METHODOLOGY

This report includes two types of analyses: changes over time (from 2006 to 2008) in the use of specialty tiers in Part D plans, and an in-depth look at specialty tiers in 2008. We used publicly available CMS files of Part D formularies to analyze plan tier structures and placement of drugs onto specialty tiers. However, these files do not clearly label specialty tiers. Thus, in 2006, 2007, and 2008, we labeled as an "apparent" all of the followingspecialty characteristics:

- The plan's highest where a plan uses a tier with cost sharingtier (or, in very over 33 percent, second-highest tier);
- Cost sharing of from 25 percent to 33 percent; and
- A small number of drugs assigned to the tier.

This process yielded a count of 1,443 PDPs with but it likely resulted in some mis-labeling of tiers. For example, in situations where additional information is available, that information shows that some plans have tiers for non-specialty injectible drugs that would have been classified as specialty tiers under this process. Conversely, specialty tiers in a small number of MA plans have flat copays that would have caused us to label the tier as non-specialty.

In 2008, we obtained from CMS additional for the 2008 plans, we were able to identify true specialty tiers and eliminate tiers for non-specialty injectibles or other non-specialty drugs when those plans provided labels. However, many plans did not provide labels and we were not able to determine whether or not their apparent specialty tiers were truly specialty tiers. As reported below, this information yielded a count of 1,262 PDPs with specialty tiers or 181 fewer than the count of "apparent" for which no information was provided in the labeling information as well as some tiers that are not "true" specialty tiers.

For the purposes of comparing the use of specialty tiers from 2006 to 2008, we have used our more general measure of "apparent" specialty tiers tiers in 2008, we used the more precise definition of and eliminated from the analysis plans that did not provide labels for their tiers.

2006-2008 COMPARISONS

Use of Specialty Tiers

Since 2006, there have been notable increases in the use of what appear to be specialty tiers. Threefourths of PDP enrollees, and nine-tenths of all MA-PD enrollees, are in a plan that uses an apparent specialty tier – up from about two-thirds of enrollees in 2006. As noted above, the count for 2008 relies on our definition of "apparent" specialty tiers, resulting in a larger count than reliance on labels supplied to CMS (but not available for all plans).

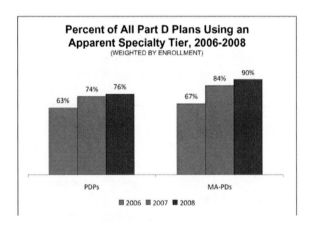

Most of the plans without a specialty tier have a structure in which a separate tier for drugs listed by other plans on a specialty tier would be redundant such as the standard benefit in law of 25 percent coinsurance for all drugs. When defined standard plans and other plans that did not fit into a clear tier structure are set aside, over nine in ten beneficiaries enrolled in tier-based plans are in plans that have a specialty tier in 2008 (92 percent of PDPs and 96 percent of MAPDs). By 2008, many of the small set of tier-based plans without specialty tiers used percentage coinsurance for most or all tiers. In these cases, specialty-tier drugs were likely to be on tiers with a similar level of coinsurance to that found in specialty tiers. But these plans differ in that there is no limitation on requests for tiering exceptions.

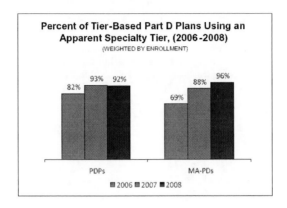

Cost Sharing

CMS limits cost sharing for specialty tiers to 25 percent, but allows plans to charge higher coinsurance if offset with other plan features, such as a lower deductible. Fewer than half of plans charge 25 percent coinsurance. Instead, half of PDPs, and slightly less than half of MA-PDs, take advantage of the flexibility offered by CMS to charge the maximum of 33 percent coinsurance for specialty-tier drugs.

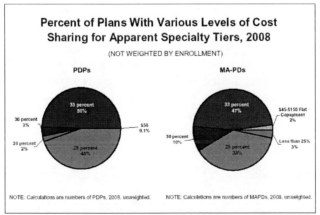

Despite these shifts, enrollment still favors plans with lower coinsurance for specialty-tier drugs. The enrollment-weighted median copay for specialty tiers has grown from 25 percent to 30 percent in PDPs, but it has remained at 25 percent for MA-PDs. MA-PDs are slightly more likely than PDPs to charge lower coinsurance for specialty tiers, including a small percentage of MA-PDs that charge less than 25 percent (including flat copays).

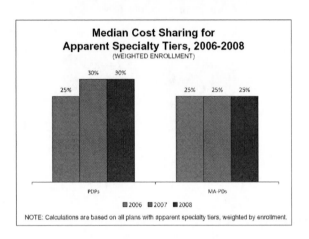

Because specialty-tier drugs are by definition very expensive, a beneficiary will reach both the coverage gap and catastrophic coverage during a full year of taking a specialty-tier drug. A beneficiary taking a $600 drug monthly for the entire year will reach the $2,510 initial coverage limit in just over four months and the catastrophic cap in about ten months; more quickly if she is taking additional drugs or a more expensive drug. Higher coinsurance during the initial coverage period will not change the timing of when the beneficiary reaches the coverage gap, because the initial coverage limit is based on total spending. If the beneficiary has paid more out of pocket before reaching the gap, however, she will reach catastrophic coverage somewhat earlier in the year – whenever she has paid $4,050 out of pocket.[1] Because the out-of-pocket threshold amount and catastrophic coverage do not vary by plan, plan cost sharing differences during the initial coverage period have little impact on total costs paid by beneficiaries by the end of the year. In four different examples (flat copayments of $25 and $50 and coinsurance of 25 percent and 33 percent) calculated for a drug priced at $1,000 per month taken all year long, total out-of-pocket costs for the year ranged only from $4,340 to $4,373.

The cost sharing amount paid by the beneficiary in the initial coverage period will affect their pattern of out-of-pocket costs from month to month, so it could have an impact on affordability to the patient her ability to continue taking the drug before or during the coverage gap. For example, a beneficiary who cannot afford the full $1,000 cost of the drug during the coverage gap may never reach catastrophic coverage. Likewise, a beneficiary who does not need to take a drug for the full year may not reach the catastrophic coverage threshold. These beneficiaries will experience larger differences in total out-of-pocket costs depending on whether they pay lower or higher cost sharing in the initial coverage period.

2008 ANALYSIS

Methodology

For this 2008 analysis, we examined data for both MA-PDs and PDPs, but saw no systematic differences between the two types of plans. Results are reported here for PDPs only. PDPs are included in this analysis only if they clearly labeled a tier as a specialty tier in 2008 (1,262 of 1,824 PDPs in 2008 fewer than the 1,443 PDPs which lty tiers inwe the previous section). We excluded any plans that did not submit tier labels or that have unusual tier designs. Many of these plans use the defined standard benefit, but some may also have specialty tiers. For example, some plans number their tiers rather than providing labels, so there is no way to tell with publicly available information which tier is officially designated a specialty tier. We also excluded "apparent" specialty tiers that were labeled by the plan as being for injectibles or Part B drugs.

As in other analysis we completed recently for MedPAC, we define a drug as a unique chemical entity, for example, combining all brand-name and generic versions of the same chemical entity.[2] Normally in our analysis of plan formularies, we also combine all forms, strengths, and package sizes of the chemical entity. For this analysis of specialty drugs, we found that dosage form but not strength or package size - affects the consideration of a drug as a specialty drug.

For many drugs, dosage form affects whether a drug is on the specialty tier (likely due to price). For example, Fentanyl (an opioid analgesic) is never a specialty drug as a patch, but it is often a specialty drug as an oral solid. Tobramycin (an antibiotic) is often a specialty drug in the inhaled form used for cystic fibrosis patients. In this analysis, e chemical entity xwe define form level. Thus, Fentanyl counts as 4 "drugs":

Dosage From for FenTanyl	Ever Specialty?
Oral Solid	Yes
Oral Other	Yes
Patch	No
Solution/Suspension/Powder	No

This strategy results in a universe of 1,493 form and chemical entity combinations, which we simply call "drugs" on the following pages. This universe represents an increase over the 1,141on the following pages separate chemical entities used in other analysis of formularies for 2008.

Number of Drugs Ever on a Specialty Tier

Most drugs (81 percent of all possible combinations of chemical entities and forms) are never placed on a specialty tier by any Part D plan. Nearly one in five drugs (291 drugs, or 19 percent) are on a specialty tier in at least one plan. However, as will be shown in a later chart, this does not mean that a fifth of all drugs are *frequently* on a specialty tier.

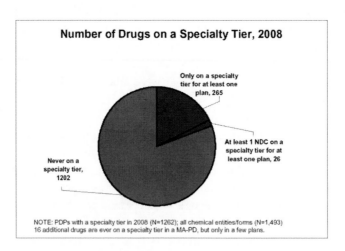

For most of these drugs (265), each plan's formulary treats all NDC codes for a drug as one unit,treat either placing them all on a specialty tier, all on a different tier, or all off the formulary. For just a small fraction of drugs (26 drugs, or fewer than 2 percent), a plan placed at least one NDC code on a specialty tier, but also placed an NDC code for that drug on a non-specialty tier. For example, there are a few drugs for which a certain strength of a drug is on a specialty tier while other strengths are not. For the purposes of the following analyses, we do not include these 26 drugs as "specialty drugs" because -specialty version when they are listedthey are always by a plan.

The following charts provide more detail on the 265 drugs that at least one plan places only on a specialty tier. We call these drugs "specialty drugs."

Listing of Specialty Tier Drugs

The average specialty drug is listed on formulary by 82 percent of PDPs in 2008. This is slightly lower than the average for non-specialty drugs, which are on formulary for an average of 86 percent of PDPs.

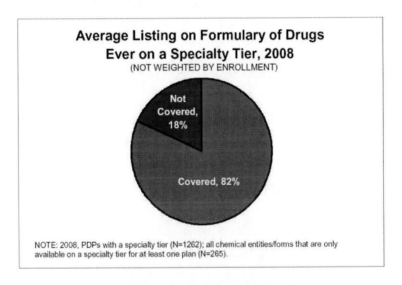

Average Listing on Formulary of Drugs Ever on a Specialty Tier, 2008
(NOT WEIGHTED BY ENROLLMENT)

Not Covered, 18%

Covered, 82%

NOTE: 2008, PDPs with a specialty tier (N=1262); all chemical entities/forms that are only available on a specialty tier for at least one plan (N=265).

Variation in Placement of Specialty Drugs on Specialty Tier

There is considerable variation in whether plans put a given drug on a specialty tier. Although we have identified 265 drugs as "specialty drugs," no one plan places all of these drugs on a specialty tier, and very few of these drugs are on a specialty tier in every plan. As discussed in the next section, these differences in tier placement can have important implications for beneficiary cost sharing.

Of the 265 specialty drugs we identified, fewer than one in five (45 drugs, or 17 percent) are placed on a specialty tier in almost all cases, that is, by more than 90 percent of plans that list them on formulary. Even among these drugs, only three (glatiramer/Copaxone, imatinib/Gleevec, and lanreotide/ Somatuline) are always on the specialty tier when listed by a plan with a specialty tier. A full list of the drugs that are placed on the specialty tier in more than 90 percent of plans appears on the following page. The list is dominated by cancer therapies and drugs for auto-immune disorders, but also includes drugs to treat AIDS, hepatitis C, and a variety of other conditions.

For other specialty drugs, there is even more variation in whether they are placed on a specialty tier when they are listed. About two in five specialty drugs (108, or 41 percent) are placed on a specialty tier by a majority of plans, but fewer than 90 percent of plans. The remaining two-fifths of specialty drugs (112 drugs, or 42 percent) are placed on a specialty tier in fewer than half of plans.

We did not collect pricing information for this project, so we are not able to determine how often proximity to the $600/month threshold may be causing this lack of uniformity in plan decisions about whether to include a drug on the specialty tier.

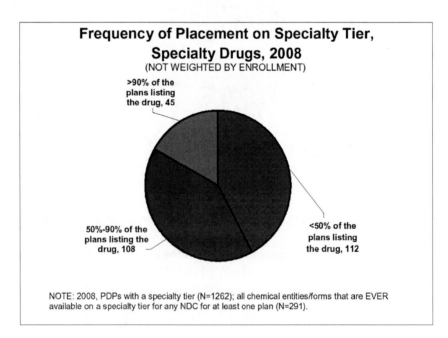

Frequency of Placement on Specialty Tier, Specialty Drugs, 2008
(NOT WEIGHTED BY ENROLLMENT)

>90% of the plans listing the drug, 45

50%-90% of the plans listing the drug, 108

<50% of the plans listing the drug, 112

NOTE: 2008, PDPs with a specialty tier (N=1262); all chemical entities/forms that are EVER available on a specialty tier for any NDC for at least one plan (N=291).

Drugs on Specialty Tier for at Least 90 Percent of Plans Listing Them

Cancer Therapy	Auto-Immune Diseases	Other Conditions
Imatinib	Infliximab (RA, psoriasis)	Cidofovir (AIDS)
Sunitinib	Abatacept (RA)	Enfuvirtide (AIDS)
Temsirolimus	Etanercept (RA, psoriasis)	Botulinum toxin A (Various)
Dasatinib	Adalimumab (RA,psoriasis)	Agalsidase (Fabry disease)
Sorafenib	Alefacept (psoriasis)	Imiglucerase (Gauchers disease)
Erlotinib	Efalizumab (psoriasis)	Immune globulin (immunodeficiency)
Aldesleukin	Natalizumab (MS, Crohns)	Pegademase (immunodeficiency)
Arsenic	Glatiramer (MS)	Interferon gamma (granulomatous
Vorinostat	Interferon beta (MS)	disease)
Sargramostim	Lenalidomide (multiple myeolma)	Interferon alfacon (hepatitis C)
Filgrastim		Interferon Alfa (HPV)
Palifermin		Palivizumab (premature infants)
Lanreotide Acetate		Ziconotide (chronic pain)
Palonosetron		Tobramycin (antibiotic)
Oprelvekin		Somatropin (pituitary stimulant)
		Treprostinil (pulmonary hypertension)
		Bosentan (pulmonary hypertension)
		Basiliximab (anti-rejection)

Tier Placement of Specialty Drugs When Not on a Specialty Tier

As shown in the previous exhibit, most drugs that appear on specialty tiers are not universally placed there by the plans that list them on formulary. For each of the 265 drugs that are placed on at least one PDP's specialty tier, we different tier.

Because of variation in plan decisions about whether to place drugs on a specialty tier, PDPs place the average specialty drug on a specialty tier just over half the time (56 percent).[3] The most important implication of this variation in tier placements is the cost sharing faced by a beneficiary for these drugs.

When plans list these drugs on formulary but do not place them on a specialty tier, they most often place the drugs on a preferred brand tier or a single tier for brand drugs (18 percent). These tiers are likely to have a flat copay; in 2008, the median copay for a preferred brand tier was $30. This amount is considerably below the coinsurance on a specialty tier, which amounts to at least $150 (25 percent coinsurance for a drug at the minimum monthly cost of $600).

It is also somewhat likely that a plan will place a specialty drug on a non-preferred tier (14 percent). These tiers most commonly have flat copays typically about $70, but in a small number of plans they have coinsurance even higher than the 25 to 33 percent coinsurance typical of specialty tiers.

Most specialty drugs are branded drugs. Thus, it is not surprising that plans with specialty tiers rarely place specialty drugs on a generic tier, but it does happen 8 percent of the time - presumably for drugs that are costly even when sold as generics. In most plans, placement on a generic tier means a very low copay, typically about $5 in 2008.

A small number of plans have additional tiers specifically for injectible drugs, drugs that are usually covered by Part B, or other special cases. These tiers often have the specialty tier. Plans place specialty drugs on these tiers only 4 percent of the time, in part because these tiers are less common.

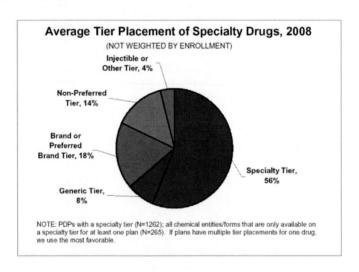

Utilization Management for Specialty Drugs

In addition to the high costs they face for specialty drugs, beneficiaries are also fairly likely to face utilization management hurdles that can delay or restrict their access to a given drug. Steps that create hurdles for beneficiaries and their physicians are viewed by plans as tools to ensure appropriate use of these expensive drugs. Specialty drugs are nearly twice as likely as other drugs to be subject to utilization management measures (37 to 38 percent vs. 20 percent). The measures flagged in CMS's are prior authorization, quantity limits, and step therapy.formulary database

The contrast is even more striking when looking specifically at the use of prior authorization. Non-specialty drugs are subject to prior authorization just 6 percent of the time when they are listed on formulary, but specialty drugs are subject to prior authorization 34 to 35 percent of the time. Because prior authorization is a labor intensive process, plans are more likely to use this tool for more expensive drugs such as those that are placed on specialty tiers.

Interestingly, specialty drugs are about equally likely to be subject to these utilization management measures regardless of whether they are on a particular plan's specialty tier. In other words, the useplan's specialty of a specialty tier seems not to preclude a appropriate use of these drugs.

	Drugs Naver on Specialty	Drugs Ever on Specialty Tier
Share of PDPs Applying Utilization Management, if Listed on Formulary:		
Not on Specialty Tier	20%	37%
On Specialty Tier		38%
Share of PDPs Applying Prior Authorization, if Listed on Formulary:		
Not on Specialty Tier	6%	34%
On Specialty Tier		35%

Characteristics of Specialty Drugs: Form

Injectible drugs are more likely than any other dosage form to be placed on a specialty tier, and the majority of specialty drugs are injectibles. Many injectibles are biologics that are costly to produce, pushing the monthly cost of these drugs over CMS's $600 minimum monthly price threshold.

Nearly a third of all injectible drugs are on a specialty tier in at least one plan, while only one in ten pills are ever placed on a specialty tier.

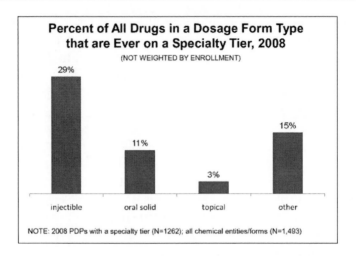

As a result of the likelihood that injectibles will be placed on a specialty tier, nearly two-thirds of specialty drugs are injectibles, even though injectibles make up closer to one-third of all drugs.

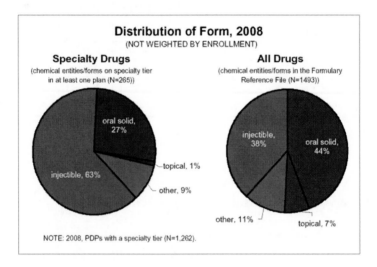

Characteristics of Specialty Drugs: Brand Status

Drugs available only as brands are much more likely than other drugs to be placed on a specialty tier, and the majority of specialty drugs are only available as brands. Drugs tend to be more expensive while they are still on patent, and many of the drugs listed on specialty tiers are fairly recent. In addition, many specialty drugs are biologics that have no pathway for direct generic competition.

Drugs only available as brands are placed on a specialty tier almost a third of the time. (Drugs with "unknown" brand status are probably brands; those labeled "mixed" have both brand and generic versions or brand and "unknown" versions.)

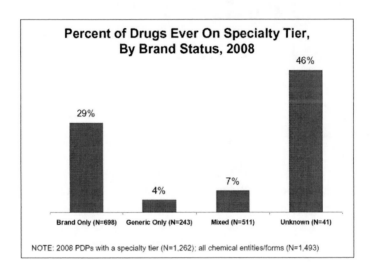

Characteristics of Specialty Drugs: Therapeutic Class

Some classes are much more likely than others to be on a specialty tier; in six classes, drugs are on a specialty tier about half the time or more. Three of those classes are relatively small: enzyme replacements and modifiers, pituitary suppressants, and blood products and modifiers (including erythropoetins, or EPO). The others are large classes that are also "protected classes" under CMS rules: antineoplastics (cancer therapies such as Gleevec) and antivirals (including HIV drugs), as well as the class of immunological drugs that includes the protected immune suppressant drugs for transplant patients. Plans are required to list on formulary most or all of the protected drugs in these classes.

Classes with drugs for many common chronic conditions (Cardiovascular, Respiratory, Gastrointestinal) are mostly not on specialty tiers.

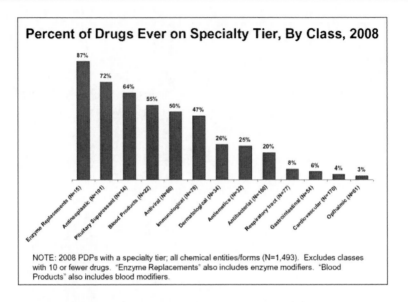

Drugs in just four classes account for nearly two-thirds of specialty drugs. These four classes include the three large classes with a high rate of placement on specialty tiers (Antineoplastics, Immunologics, and Antivirals), as well as Antibacterials, a very large class whose drugs are placed on a specialty tier about 20 percent of the time. Antineoplastics alone make up over a quarter of all specialty drugs.

Although they make up a large share of specialty drugs, these four classes make up only a fourth of all drugs.

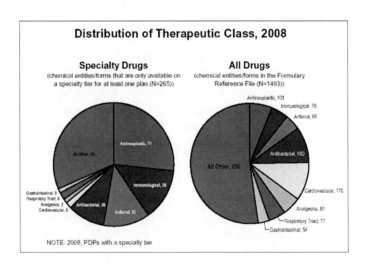

End Notes

[1] Initial coverage limit and catastrophic threshold amounts are for 2008.

[2] Jack Hoadley, Elizabeth Hargrave, Katie Merrell and Lan Zhao, "*Medicare Part D Benefit Designs and Formularies, 2006-2009,*" presentation to MedPAC, December 5, 2008.

[3] The numbers shown in the chart represent averages, calculated across the 265 drugs that are ever on a specialty tier, of the percentage of plans placing each drug on a particular tier. Averages are not weighted by enrollment.

CHAPTER SOURCES

The following chapters were previously published:

Chapter 1 – This is an edited reformatted and augmented version of a Congressional Research Service publication, report R40611, dated June 1, 2009.

Chapter 2 – This is an edited reformatted and augmented version of a Congressional Budget Office publication, dated September 2010.

Chapter 3 – This is an edited reformatted and augmented version of a Havard Medical School for the Medicare Payment Advisory Commission publication, report 10-4, dated May 2010

Chapter 4 – This is an edited reformatted and augmented version of a NORC at the University of Chicago and Georgetown University for the Medicare Payment Advisory Commission publication, report 09-1, dated February 2009.

INDEX